SOUTHERN LITERARY STUDIES

SOUTHERN LITERARY STUDIES

Edited by
LOUIS D. RUBIN, JR.

A Season of Dreams: The Fiction of Eudora Welty
BY ALFRED APPEL, JR.

The Hero with the Private Parts
ESSAYS BY ANDREW LYTLE

Hunting in the Old South

Hunting in the Old South

Original Narratives of the Hunters

SELECTED AND EDITED BY
Clarence Gohdes

LOUISIANA STATE UNIVERSITY PRESS   Baton Rouge

Copyright © 1967 by
Louisiana State University Press

Library of Congress Catalogue Card Number 67–13895
Printed in the United States of America by
Kingsport Press, Inc., Kingsport, Tennessee
Designed by Jules B. McKee
ISBN 0-8071-2517-2 (pbk)

To my brother OTTO C. GOHDES

Preface

THE history of hunting in the United States has attracted comparatively little attention from professional historians, and, therefore, I offer this collection of stories as a kind of source book for further studies of the subject. Although I have done considerable research on hunting in the Old South and, for example, have read the laws pertaining to game, etc., in the published statutes of the Southern states prior to the Civil War, I have shaped this book not so much for the benefit of students of history as for the delectation of readers like myself who enjoy hunting yarns simply for their own sake. Accordingly, this collection is aimed at hunters who like to read about the other fellow's adventures in the good old days, when the supply of game seemed unlimited and field sports were an essential part of everyday life.

The volume consists of narratives and descriptions of hunting in the Southern states prior to the Civil War. In that era the region was commonly considered to harbor the most enthusiastic devotees of the sport in the United States, and hunters from the North and from Europe felt lucky indeed when the opportunity presented itself to accept an invitation from a planter to take part in the chase. The material is derived from a variety of magazines and books, and the writers range from professional journalists to sportsmen who merely wrote letters to periodicals concerned with agriculture or the turf. My purpose, which guided the choice of selections, has been to illustrate the areas and methods involved in bagging the various sorts of game commonly pursued, from bear and deer to wildfowl and varmints. The arrangement is informal. One may browse at will. The chapters have been provided with brief introductions in which I have sometimes undertaken to call attention to the general features of the kind of hunt illustrated and, where possible, to give the reader a little pertinent information about the individuals who penned the screeds.

PREFACE

The tales assembled here have been previously serialized in the *Georgia Review*, beginning with the fall issue of 1964, and are reprinted with the permission of its editor, William Wallace Davidson, whose family has numbered a long line of hunters, as well as distinguished students of the South. I have been encouraged in my efforts to search out authentic accounts by the enthusiastic response of Donald K. Adams, the best turkey hunter on the faculty of Duke University, and by my brother Otto C. Gohdes, with whom as a young boy I first took to the field with my father's old shotgun in pursuit of rabbits. I have been directed to certain sources by the late Charles S. Sydnor and by my dear friend Jay B. Hubbell, whose knowledge of the Old South extends far beyond the realm of its literary authors. My neighbor Robert Woody has also put his immense knowledge of life in the Old South at my disposal.

Some of the selections have been excerpted from longer accounts, but for the most part they represent the original entities. Here and there I have doctored the punctuation, etc.; otherwise, the texts are faithfully reproduced.

I am grateful to Louis D. Rubin, of Hollins College, for first suggesting the possibility of bringing out these yarns and sketches in book form; and to the staff of the Louisiana State University Press for their expert collaboration. Mrs. Ruth B. Hubert has been especially kind in improving my manuscript and in rounding up appropriate illustrations.

CLARENCE GOHDES

Duke University
March, 1967

Introduction

THE following accounts of hunts in the antebellum South have been selected with the purpose of illustrating the variety and method of the field sports of the time through more or less authentic narratives written by the hunters themselves. I say "more or less authentic," for what Nimrod ever described a coup without a little garnishing? Of course an old-fashioned flavor attaches itself to the style of writing employed by these sportsmen, but I have not tampered with it editorially, because it seems to add a touch—often a very leisurely air—which helps to recapture the spirit of the old regime.

While the literary, the political, the economic, and even the scientific interests of the prewar planters have been studied, except for fox hunting, the field sports of the Old South have been neglected by historians. Perhaps the reason is natural enough, since everyone knows that hunting with gun and dog, and sometimes with horse, was as common in all sections of the country as butchering hogs or building the morning fire. Moreover, the eyes of Americans were constantly shifting westward as the newer frontiers were opened, and consequently it has been forgotten that in the generation prior to 1860 the South—and not the West—really provided the ideal place to enjoy a hunt in true sportsman's style.

The reasons for Southern pre-eminence were simple enough. The section had a marked advantage when compared with the older Northern states in including a vast region of coastal and river swamp plus an extensive mountainous area both of which provided the best sort of cover for game. It embraced the chief wintering ground in the country for migratory wildfowl, and it had a relatively thin population. And, above all, the South justly claimed at the top of its social ladder the largest group of rural residents in the United States who were possessed of both wealth and leisure. Although long before 1860 sportsmen above the level of pothunters were repeating Horace Greeley's advice to go West, the connoisseurs recognized the eminence of the South. For example, an English authority on American hunting, Captain Flack, in 1866 stated his opinion that prior to the war the Southern planters indulged "more than any other Americans in the wild sports of the forest and prairie," and Frank Forester (Henry William Herbert), foremost authority on hunting during the mid-century, dedicated his chief work, *The Field Sports of the United States,* to Colonel Wade Hampton of South Carolina as a "tribute of homage to the First Sportsman in the land." In his description of deer hunting in the United States Forester declared:

> In order . . . to enjoy Deer-hunting in anything like perfection—for, after all, here, to the Northward, it is practised ninety-nine times out of a hundred as it is in the West—I had almost said altogether as a means of obtaining venison, and not for the sport's sake—we must go into Virginia, into the Carolinas, Louisiana and Mississippi. There we find the gentlemen of the land, not pent up in cities, but dwelling on their estates; there we find hunters, *par amours,* if I may so express myself, and packs of hounds maintained regularly, and hunted with all legitimate accompaniments of well-blown bugle and well-whooped halloo; with mounted cavaliers, fearlessly riding through brush, through briar, over flood, over mire . . . as desperately, for the first blood, or the kill, as they do in old England, in Leicester or Northampton, to the Quorn hounds, or the Squire's lady pack. This is *the Sport,* par excellence.

That Forester knew what he was talking about cannot be questioned, for he had been brought up as the younger son of a fine old English sporting family and was an ardent enthusiast long before he ever came to New York. We may even call upon folklore to attest to the merits of hunting in the South by reminding the reader that the outstanding hunter in American legend was a Southerner—Daniel Boone. And Davy Crockett may be thrown into the bargain.

There is a possibility, we might add, that something of the reputation for hospitality which the South acquired, and which Olmsted tried in vain to undermine, was due to the royal entertainment provided visiting sportsmen during their frequent sojourns in the section for the purpose of chasing the fox or the deer. There is no need for surprise in stumbling upon the records of hunting societies like the Camden Hunting Club of Georgia, established in 1827, whose members rode out in official uniform, scarlet coats, and whose rules and regulations included the following: "Any member who shall fire at a deer less than forty yards distant and not *hit* or *kill*, when the *opportunity is fair*, shall be fined. No deer shall be considered hit unless *killed*, or unless *blood is seen*." Neighboring clubs often vied with each other, the losers paying the costs of a dinner with wines or a barbecue with brandy or whiskey. There were those who even hunted with the lance, in the choicest Central-European style.

Though the South had its gentlemen hunters like Wade Hampton, all down the line of its social ranks it had devotees of the sport. The small farmer, the frontiersman, the poor white—and frequently the Negro—all were hunters. As Audubon remarked of the Kentuckians known to him, their guns were often "the means of providing their subsistence" and "the source of their principal sports and pleasures." Important, too, in the old days were the professionals who supplied the meat markets of towns and cities. In Texas during the 1850's one received a dollar for a "good fat buck's haunch," the same price for a turkey cock, fifty cents for a hen turkey or a small haunch of doe venison, while grouse and wild ducks (widgeons) brought a quarter apiece.

Though deer and bear provided the chief big-game sport, and wild cat ("panther") or wolf hunting was fairly common in many localities long afterward, in the decades before 1860 there seems to have been an occasional buffalo in the wilder parts of Kentucky and elsewhere in the South, although most of the few that remained were in gentlemen's parks and wore bells around their necks. The Southwest, of course, provided game more commonly associated with the region beyond the Mississippi River, but elk were still to be found in Virginia, Tennessee, and Louisiana. There is a fairly authentic record of a gigantic elk killed near Roundaway Bayou during the period—gross weight 704 pounds, length from tip of the nose to the hinder hoof, eleven feet, and height at the withers sixteen hands—a record-breaker, indeed.

In 1857 a Philadelphia expert expressed the opinion that the best quail shooting known to him was to be found in the neighborhood of

Lynchburg, Virginia, where a good marksman, he said, could bag a hundred in one day. But the professionals, who trapped the birds in great cylindrical nets by "driving" them with horses, often beat that record, if we may judge by the numerous crates of live quail sent to the city markets. In the forties a determined turkey hunter, like Poe's friend, Philip Pendleton Cooke, managed to bag twenty or more of the big birds per season in or near the Shenandoah Valley, but in the central part of the state Northern sportsmen usually found they were "so very wild that little or no inducement was offered to hunt them." All were agreed, however, that turkeys were to be found in "some abundance" in the wilder portions of Tennessee, Arkansas, Louisiana, Mississippi, Alabama, and Florida, and in certain oases in the other Southern states, especially in Texas. When the railroads issued hunting and fishing guides to encourage travel during the 1870's, turkeys, along with deer and bear, were featured for most of the Southern region.

In the 1840's, with a Negro to hold a fire-pan, one could sometimes obtain as many as a hundred woodcocks during a single night in parts of Louisiana, but near Charleston, South Carolina, with more orthodox methods five or six brace were thought to constitute a very good bag. In St. Tammany Parish, the Creoles were especially fond of a small bird called the *grussée,* and pothunters there and elsewhere regularly pursued magnolia birds, robins, or other feathered creatures now on the songbird list. Cranes and swans were pretty generally shot, along with ducks and geese; and wild pigeons were still plentiful, especially, it seems, in Kentucky and Alabama.

Of course, long before the War Between the States many a Southern locality was practically barren of good hunting. Even in the eighteenth century, the diaries of William Byrd disclose, the deer had disappeared from the area near Westover, Virginia, and when venison was sent eastward from a remoter plantation that gentleman considered it a treat sufficiently worthy to serve as a present to the Governor in Williamsburg. Byrd records the bad luck which occasionally attended quail shooting on his home property but seems to have been fairly regularly supplied with blue-winged teal. In his latest journal, however, pigeon appears to have been the chief substitute for blue-wing—and possibly that was of the *passenger* variety. A scarcity of deer in parts of Virginia and the Carolinas was occasionally a matter of concern even in Colonial times, for among the earliest game laws of the region there are a number which deal with a closed season.

As everybody knows, effective legislation on hunting has been a very recent item in the legal history of our states, and as a consequence there is a common belief that prior to 1860 there were no game laws at all; but such is not the case. For example, in 1699 the statutes of Virginia made it illegal to kill or buy a deer from the Indians between the first of February and the last of July, the fine being five hundred pounds of tobacco, or thirty lashes if the offender was a slave. In those days one-half of the fine went to the local church; the other to the informer whose testimony secured the conviction. In 1734 the closed season on deer ran from the first of January to the last of August; but various modifications were made, and exceptions, too, for the revised statutes exempted the area west of the mountains and allowed the frontier residents to kill for food at any time. In 1860 the season was closed from January 15 to July 15, and the fine for a violation was set at ten dollars. Tame deer with a bell or collar were protected, but one was allowed to hunt in his own private park at any time. As for wildfowl, long before 1860 Virginia law forbade shooting from boats or floats after sundown, private marshes excepted. There was, moreover, to be no fowling with "any gun which cannot be conveniently discharged from the shoulder at arm's length without a rest."

In North Carolina in 1735 the closed season on deer extended from February 15 to July 15, with a fine of five pounds for violation. Ten years later the regulation was amended so as to make the fine applicable to the mere possessor of venison or of green hides during the closed season. No one was permitted to pursue game in the "King's Waste" within the province unless he could show that he had planted and tended five thousand hills of corn, spaced five feet apart, in the county in which he purposed to hunt. By the 1850's deer were protected from February 20 to August 15, though anyone was allowed to hunt on his own property.

Most of the newer Southern states, however, seem to have had no closed season at all; yet there is reason to believe that there were gentlemen's agreements to refrain from hunting in certain favorite resorts until a specified day. County restrictions also existed.

References in the laws to penalties for infractions by slaves, differing from the fines imposed upon the whites, indicate that hunting was not confined to the ruling race. And when the fear of insurrection made the possession of firearms by Negroes a legal offense, the regulations were often disregarded, especially during the hunting season, just as the statutes prohibiting the teaching of slaves to read and write were liberally ignored. A farmer possessed of one or two slaves was as likely to take to the field in their company as he was to join his neighbors in the pursuit of game. Moreover, slaves who wished to add to the larder by shooting rabbits and squirrels, or even nobler quarry, were certainly not discouraged. On certain plantations the first law of nature must have made the foraging for meat a necessity, if Thomas Nuttall's account of the common allowance for feeding slaves at Pointe Coupée in 1820—about one quart of corn a day—bears any resemblance to the truth. Among both blacks and whites pothunting was the rule. In case of illness in the family fresh meat was generally considered beneficial to the patient, and slaves were often sent out to procure it. To this day in the mountainous sections squirrel stew is favored for this purpose.

In more formally arranged hunts, however, where several planters or guests from a distance participated, the Negroes usually took subordinate positions as grooms or beaters and porters of the quarry. But in many localities certain Negroes or Indians were numbered among the expert Nimrods of the community, and their society was at times apparently courted. Long before the advent of Jack Johnson and Willie Mays, hunting was a factor which promoted integration.

Field sports in the Old South were men's business, and ladies seem to have been left at home, even when there was riding to hounds. Of course many a farmer's wife was capable of ridding the hen roost or the sheepfold of an invading varmint, or of bringing down a turkey gobbler following a trail of corn set out to bait him within range of her home. But the distaff connection with game was chiefly confined to the kitchen. A sporadic glance through cook books emanating from the South before the Civil War reveals little special interest in game, wild ducks and pigeons being the chief exceptions, as recipes for their preparation are fairly common. However, Mrs. Mary Randolph's *Virginia House-Wife,* which went into a fourth edition in 1830, contained the following instructions on roasting woodcocks or snipes:

INTRODUCTION xvii

> Pluck, but don't draw them, put them on a small spit, dredge and baste them well with lard, toast a few slices of bread, put them on a clean plate, and set it under the birds while they are roasting; if the fire be good, they will take about ten minutes; when you take them from the spit, lay them upon the toasts on the dish, pour melted butter round them, and serve them up.

And *Housekeeping in the Blue Grass,* prepared by the Ladies of the Presbyterian Church of Paris, Kentucky, in its tenth edition by 1874, starts off its section on meats with this recipe for cooking a saddle of venison:

> Put the venison on to bake, with the side which is uppermost when it comes to the table next to the pan; then make the dressing thus: with the fingers crumble a small piece of light bread, which season highly with pepper and salt. When the meat is about half done, turn it over, and cut on either side of the bone several places, about two and a half inches long, which stuff with the dressing just made. Then pour all over the meat a half tea-cupful of catsup. Into a half tea-cup of black molasses stir a table-spoonful of whole allspice, and a tea-spoonful of brown sugar; this, too, pour over the meat; then crumble light bread all over the upper surface, keeping the meat well basted all the while, and cooking slowly, for it burns readily. Just before taking the venison off, put here and there all over it a little jelly.

Something of the problem besetting the preservation of game in the good old days is suggested by the following item on "Preserving Meat without Salt" which appeared in the *Confederate Receipt Book* (Richmond, 1863), the only known recipe book published during the life of the Confederacy:

> We need salt as a relish to our food, but it is not essential in the preservation of our meats. The Indians used little or no salt, yet they preserved meat and even fish in abundance by drying. This can be accomplished by fire, by smoke, or by sunshine, but the most rapid and reliable mode is by all of these agents combined. To do this select a spot having fullest command of sunshine. Erect there a wigwam five or six feet high, with an open top, in size proportioned to the quantity of meat to be cured, and protected from the winds, so that all the smoke must pass through the open top. The meat cut into pieces suitable for drying (the thinner the better) to be suspended

on rods in the open comb, and a vigorous smoke made of decayed wood is to be kept up without cessation. Exposed thus to the combined influence of sunshine, heat and smoke, meat cut into slices not over an inch thick can be thoroughly cured in twenty-four hours. For thicker pieces there must be, of course, a longer time, and the curing of oily meat, such as pork, is more difficult than that of beef, venison or mutton. To cure meat in the sun hang it on the South side of your house, as near to the wall as possible without touching.

One might avoid the blowflies by peppering the venison liberally, hanging it by a rope down the well, or putting it on a hook in the smokehouse, but it was often eaten when it was more than a little "high."

The recording of hunting in the Old South was done by a variety of scribes, for the most part journalists, travellers, visiting sportsmen from the North or from Europe, and, to a lesser extent, the planters themselves. It is often said that these last, the dominant class in the regional society, failed to leave a record of themselves in print. And the only periodical known to have been printed on a plantation was one published by Joseph Addison Turner, near Eatonton, Georgia. But, as the present volume attests, the gentry at times reported on their exploits with horse, gun, and dog in letters sent to various journals which specialized in news of the turf and of hunting.

The image of the section projected in the old screeds on field sports is more allied with the moonlight and magnolias tradition than it is with the one developed in *Uncle Tom's Cabin* and the flock of novels which used the "peculiar institution" of slavery as the representative center of the picture. The sportsman's Old South was indeed a delightful realm, with a plenitude of game that now seems almost unbelievable and a leisure class at the top which took to the field as a pleasant amusement to be cherished for itself and shared with one's friends. Though modified, to be sure, something of the image survives, for the South is, comparatively, still a sportsman's paradise, not only for the hunter and the fisherman but for the golfer and Kentucky Derby fan as well.

Contents

Preface	ix
Introduction	xi
A Day at Chee-Ha	3
Turkey Hunts in Texas	11
The Virginian Canaan	31
Wild Cattle Hunting on Green Island	64
Spearing a Wild Bull	77
Pitting of Wolves	80
Possum-Hunting in Alabama	87
A Duck Hunt in Florida	94
Ibis Shooting in Louisiana	101
Woodcock Fire-Hunting	113
Deer Hunting in the Yazoo Swamp	120
Shooting Extraordinary	125
Hawking in Fairfax, Virginia	131
Miseries of a Sportsman's Wife	135
Fox Hunt	139
Deer Hunting	148
Davy Crockett Shoots Bears	153
Mike Hooter's Bar Story	160
A Bear Hunt in the Iron Mountain	165
Bear Hunt in Louisiana	171

Hunting in the Old South

A Day at Chee-Ha

WILLIAM ELLIOTT

The frequent and consistent reference to it made in the old game laws proves that deer hunting was the top-ranked field sport of the Old South. It is fitting, therefore, that this volume's first selection should describe a stag hunt. Its author, William Elliott (1788–1863), was a planter of noblest South Carolina breed, though educated at Harvard and a Unionist. In letters to the Charleston *Courier,* signed "Venator" or "Piscator," he told of adventures while hunting in the pines or sedge fields, or while fishing off Hilton Head and Port Royal Sound. His encounter with a monstrous devil-fish, which after being harpooned dragged him in a dory for twenty miles or more, made headlines and pictures in the London *Illustrated News* and was only one of the reasons for his becoming the most widely read authority on Southern sports during his day. When his yarns were collected as *Carolina Sports by Land and Water* (1846), the book soon took the place which it still holds as the classic account of the subject. It was popular in England as well as at home and was several times reprinted.

Among the readers was Henry Thoreau, who quoted lengthy extracts with comments in his journal for February 21, 1861. The captious Henry noted examples of inconsistency and cruelty exhibited by Elliott but admitted him to the category of "a regular sportsman" who described his hunting "with great zest" and whose motive was "not profit or subsistence, but sport." As one of the examples of cruelty Thoreau cited Elliott's attempt to run a wounded deer down with a horse—an incident that appears in this narrative.

THE traveller in South Carolina, who passes along the road between the Ashepoo and Combahee rivers will be struck by the appearance of two lofty white columns, rising among the pines that skirt the road. They are the only survivors of eight, which supported, in times anterior to our revolutionary war, a sylvan temple, erected by a gentleman,* who to the higher qualities of a devoted patriot, united the taste and liberality of the sportsman. The spot was admirably chosen, being on the brow of a piney ridge, which slopes away at a long gun-shot's length into a thick swamp; and many a deer has, we doubt not, in times past, been shot from the temple when it stood in its pride—as we ourselves have struck them from its ruins. From this ruin, stretching eastwardly some twelve or fourteen miles, is a neck of land, known from the Indian name of the small river that waters and almost bisects it, as Chee-ha—or, as it is incorrectly written, Chy-haw! It is now the best hunting-ground in Carolina—for which the following reasons may be given. The lands are distributed in large tracts; there are therefore few proprietors. The rich land is confined to the belt of the rivers, and there remains a wide expanse of barrens, traversed by deep swamps, always difficult and sometimes impassable, in which the deer find a secure retreat.

At a small hunting-lodge located in this region, it has often been my good fortune to meet a select body of hunting friends, and enjoy in their company the pleasure of the chase.

I give you one of my "days"—not that the success was unusual, it was by no means so; but that it was somewhat more marked by incident than most of its fellows. We turned out, *after breakfast,* on a fine day in February, with a pack of twelve hounds, and two whippers in, or drivers, as we call them. The field consisted of one old shot besides myself, and two sportsmen who had not yet "fleshed their maiden swords." When we reached the ground, we had to experience the fate which all tardy sportsmen deserve, and must often undergo: the fresh print of dogs' feet, and the deep impression of horses' hoofs, showed us that another party had anticipated us in the drive, and that the game had been started and was off. Two expedients suggested themselves—we must either leave our ground, and in that case incur the risk of sharing the same fate in our next drive; or, we must beat up the ground now before us in a way which our predecessors in the field had probably

---

* Col. Barnard Elliott.

neglected to do. We chose the latter part: and finding that the drive embraced two descriptions of ground—first, the main wood, which we inferred had already been taken, and next, the briery thickets that skirted a contiguous old field—into these thickets we pushed. Nor had we entered far, before the long, deep, querulous note of "Ruler," as he challenged on a trail, told us to expect the game. A few minutes later, and the whole pack announced the still more exciting fact—"the game is up." The first move of the deer was into a back-water, which he crossed, while the pack, half swimming, half wading, came yelping at his heels. He next dashed across an old field and made for a thicket, which he entered; it was a piece of briery and tangled ground, which the dogs could not traverse without infinite toil. By these two moves, he gained a great start of the hounds: if he kept on, we were thrown out, and our dogs lost for the day—if he doubled, and the nature of the ground favored that supposition, there were two points whereat he would be most likely to be intercepted. I consulted the wind, and made my choice. I was wrong. It proved to be a young deer, who did not need the wind, and he made for the pass I had *not selected*. The pack now turned; we found from their cry, that the deer had doubled, and our hearts beat high with expectation, as mounted on our respective hunters, we stretched ourselves across the old field which he must necessarily traverse, before he could regain the shelter of the wood. And now I saw my veteran comrade stretch his neck as if he spied something in the thicket; then with a sudden fling he brought his double barrel to his shoulder and fired. His horse, admonished by the spur, then fetched a caracole; from the new position, a new glimpse of the deer is gained—and crack! goes the second barrel. In a few moments, I saw one of our recruits dismount and fire. Soon after, the deer made his appearance and approached the second, who descended from his horse and fired. The deer kept on seemingly untouched, and had gained the crown of the hill when his second barrel brought him to the ground in sight of the whole field. We all rode to the spot, to congratulate our novice on his first exploit in sylvan warfare—when, as he stooped to examine the direction of his shot, our friend Loveleap slipped his knife into the throat of the deer, and before his purpose could be guessed at, bathed his face with the blood of his victim. (This, you must know, *is hunter's law* with

us, on the killing a first deer). As our young sportsman started up from the ablution—his face glaring like an Indian chief's in all the splendor of war-paint—Robin the hunter touched his cap and thus accosted him:

"Maussa Tickle, if you wash off dat blood dis day—you neber hab luck again so long as you hunt."

"Wash it off!" cried we all, with one accord; "who ever heard of such a folly. He can be no true sportsman, who is ashamed of such a livery."

Thus beset, and moved thereunto, by other sage advices showered upon him by his companions in sport, he wore his bloody mask to the close of that long day's sport, and sooth to say, returned to receive the congratulations of his young and lovely wife, his face still adorned with the stains of victory. Whether he was received, as victors are wont to be, returning from other fields of blood, is a point whereon I shall refuse to satisfy the impertinent curiosity of my reader; but I am bound, in deference to historic truth, to add—that the claims of our novice, to the merit and penalties of this day's hunt, were equally incomplete, for it appeared on after inspection, that Loveleap had given the mortal wound, and that Tickle had merely given the "coup de grâce" to a deer, that, if unfired on, would have fallen of itself, in a run of a hundred yards. It must be believed, however, that we were quite too generous to divulge this unpleasant discovery to our novice, in the first pride of his triumph!

And now we tried other grounds, which our precursors in the field had already beaten; so that the prime of the day was wasted before we made another start. At last, in the afternoon, a splendid burst from the whole pack made us aware that a second deer had suddenly been roused. I was riding to reach a pass (or *stand* as we term it), when I saw a buck dashing along before the hounds at the top of his speed; the distance was seventy-five yards—but I reined in my horse and let slip at him. To my surprise, he fell; but before I could reach the spot, from which I was separated by a thick underwood, he had shuffled off and disappeared. The hounds came roaring on, and showed me by their course that he had made for a marsh that lay hard by. For that we all pushed in hopes of anticipating him. He was before us, we saw him plunge into the canal, and mount the opposite bank, though evidently in distress and crippled in one of his hind legs. The dogs rush furiously on (the scent of blood in their nostrils), plunge into the canal, sweep over the bank, and soon pursuers and pursued are shut out from sight, as they wind among the thick covers that lie scattered over the face of the marsh.

"What use of horse now!" said Robin, as (sliding from his saddle where his horse instinctively made a dead halt at the edge of the impracticable Serbonian bog that lay before him) he began to climb a tree that overlooked the field of action—"what use of horse now?"

From this "vantage ground," however, he looked in vain to catch a glimpse of the deer. The eye of a lynx could not penetrate the thick mass of grass, that stretched upward six feet from the surface of the marsh. The cry of the hounds now grew faint from distance, and now again came swelling on the breeze; when suddenly our ears were saluted by a full burst from the whole pack, in that loud, open note, which tells a practised ear that the cry comes from the water.

"Zounds, Robin!" cried I, in the excitement of the moment, "they have him at bay there—there in the canal. Down from your perch, my lad, or they'll eat him, horns and all, before you reach him."

Robin apparently did not partake of this enthusiasm, for he maintained his perch on the tree, and coolly observed—"What use, maussa? fore I git dere, dem dog polish ebery bone."

"You are afraid, you rascal! you have only to swim the canal and then"—

"Got maussa," said Robin, as he looked ruefully over the field of his proposed missionary labors; "if he be water, I swim 'um—if he be bog, I bog 'um—if he be brier—I kratch tru 'um—but who de debble, but otter, no so alligator, go tru all tree one time!"

The thought was just stealing its way into my mind, that under the excitement of my feelings, I was giving an order that I might have hesitated personally to execute, when the cry of the hounds, lately so clamorous, totally ceased. "There," cried I, in the disappointed tone of a sportsman who had lost a fine buck, "save your skin, you loitering rascal! You may sleep where you sit, for by this time they have eaten him sure enough." This conclusion was soon overset by the solitary cry of Ruler, which was now heard, half a mile to the left of the scene of the late uproar.

"Again! What is this? *It is* the cry of Ruler! ho! I understand it—the deer is not eaten, but has taken to the canal—and the nose of that prince of hounds has scented him down the running stream.—Aye, aye, he makes for the woods—and now to cut him off." No sooner said than done. I gave the spur to my horse, and shot off accordingly; but not in time to prevent the success of the masterly manoeuvre by which the buck, baffling his pursuers, was now seen straining every nerve to regain the shelter of the wood. I made a desperate effort to cut him off, but reached the wood only in time to note the direction he had taken. It was now sunset, and the white, outspread tail of the deer was my only guide in the pursuit, as he glided among the trees. "Now for it, Boxer—show your speed, my gallant nag." The horse, as if he entered fully into the purpose of his rider, stretched himself to the utmost, obedient to the slightest touch of the reins, as he threaded the intricacies of the forest; and was gaining rapidly on the deer, when plash! he came to a dead halt—his fore legs plunged in a quagmire, over which the buck with his split hoofs had bounded in security. What a baulk! "but here goes"—and the gun was brought instantly to the shoulder, and the left-hand barrel fired. The distance was eighty yards, and the shot ineffectual. Making a slight circuit to avoid the bog, I again push at the deer and again approach. "Ah, if I had but reserved the charge I had so idly wasted!" But no matter, I must run him down—and gaining a position on his flank, I spurred my horse full upon his broad-side, to bear him to the ground. The noble animal (he *was* a noble animal, for he traced, with some baser admixture indeed, through Boxer, Medley, Gimcrack, to the Godolphin Arabian) refused to trample on his fellow quadruped; and, in spite of the goading spur, ranged up close along side of the buck, as if his only pride lay in surpassing him in speed. This brought me in close contact with the buck. Detaching my right foot from the stirrup, I struck the armed heel of my boot full against his head; he reeled from the blow and plunged into a neighboring thicket —too close for horse to enter. I fling myself from my horse, and pursue on foot—he gains on me; I dash down my now useless gun, and, freed from all encumbrance, press after the panting animal. A large, fallen oak lies across his path; he gathers himself up for the leap, and falls exhausted directly across it. Before he could recover his legs, and while he lay thus poised on the tree, I fling myself at full length upon the body of the struggling deer—my left hand clasps his neck, while my right detaches the knife whose fatal blade, in another moment, is buried in his throat. There he lay in his blood, and I remained sole occupant of the field. I seize my horn, but am utterly breathless, and incapable of sounding it: I strive to shout, but my voice is extinct from fatigue and exhaustion. I retrace my steps, while the waning light yet sufficed to show me the track of the deer—recover my horse and gun, and return to the tree where my victim lay. But how apprise my comrades of my position? My last shot, however, had not been unnoted—and soon their voices are heard cheering on "Ruler," while far in advance of the yet baffled pack, he follows unerringly on the tracks of the deer. They came at last but found me still so exhausted from fatigue, that to wave my bloody knife, and point to the victim where he lay at my feet, were all the history I could then give of the spirit-stirring incidents I have just recorded. Other hunting matches have I been engaged in, wherein double the number of deer have been killed; but never have I engaged in one of deeper and more absorbing interest, than that which marked this "day at Chee-ha."*

* William Elliott, *Carolina Sports by Land and Water,* London, 1867, pp. 170–180.

Turkey Hunts in Texas

CAPTAIN FLACK

In England, next to William Elliott, the best-known writer on Southern hunting was a certain Captain Flack, who had spent a number of years in the South, especially in Texas, and after returning to London contributed a series of yarns to the sporting journals under the pen name "The Ranger." In 1866 he published a book entitled *A Hunter's Experiences in the Southern States of America,* which commanded no little respect in his native land even though a portion of the contents was lifted from the earlier volumes of *Harper's Magazine.* But, despite the pilfering, Flack's work offers a good deal of information on sport in Texas. His chief enthusiasm seems to have been aroused by turkey hunting, and, consequently, a selection dealing with the pursuit of that particular variety of game has been chosen from his 1866 volume. Since a number of British sportsmen came to hunt in the South from time to time, it may be that the Appendix of *A Hunter's Experiences* served a useful purpose, for in it the author gave explicit instructions for the prospective European huntsman, arguing, incidentally, that the expenses involved in a trip to the South could be met with 250 pounds, comparatively "no money at all to men who hire a Scotch moor for 600 pounds per season." He added, "I need not say that in variety, quantity, and quality of game, the Texas country exceeds Scotland, to say nothing of the climate."

THE wild turkey seems filled with the instinct of self-preservation, being the shyest and wariest of all game found in the American continent. In districts where the foot of hunter has rarely trod, and where, consequently, the birds are comparatively unmolested, he who goes in pursuit of them must possess some knowledge of the habits of the bird and its usual haunts if he hopes for success. But where the haunts of the turkey are surrounded by plantations, they become so wild, from being so frequently hunted, that it is almost impossible for the hunter to get within gunshot. Only a veteran in the art has any chance of success. It is recorded of an old hunter that he once chased a turkey regularly for three years, only catching sight of the bird twice, although he used the 'call' with which they imitate the cry of the female, and so allure the cock within range of the rifle. But let him relate his adventures himself.

"I always hunted that ar' gobbler in the same range till I know'd his track and his 'yelp' as well as I do my old dogs. But the critter were so knowin' that when I 'called' he would run from me, *taking the opposite direction to my footmarks.*

"The old scaly varmint kept pretty much about a ridge, at the end of which, where it lost itself in the swamp, was a hollow cypress tree. Now, I *were* determined to have that gobbler, boys; so what do I do but *put on my shoes heels foremost,* walk down the hill very quietly, and get into the hollow tree. Well then I gave a call; and, boys, it would have done your hearts good to see that turkey come trotting down the ridge towards me, looking at my tracks, and *thinking I had gone the other way.*"

It is not so difficult to kill the birds before they are full grown; and the European hunter would find it a good preparation for the more serious sport of killing adult gobblers, to practise on those which have attained rather more than half their growth. By commencing with these youngsters during the latter part of August, and continuing to shoot during the autumn months, something may be learnt of the peculiarities of the bird.

Soon after I first landed at Galveston, in Texas, I took a passage in a boat which brought cord-wood for fuel from the mainland, for the purpose of having a look at the country; and after a voyage of about sixty miles over the bay we entered a sluggish stream called Cedar Bayou.

The bayou was about fifty yards wide, clear and deep. Huge trees grew up on either side, casting such a gloomy shadow on the water that it appeared black, although when dipped up in a pail it proved clear as crystal. The course of the river was very winding, and the breeze being kept off by the forest, it was necessary to pole the boat eight or ten miles up to the yard where the cordwood was to be obtained; and as it was nearly evening when we entered the bayou, the captain determined to moor her to the bank for the night, and pole up in the morning.

But that, of course, was no business of mine. So while our worthy German skipper was preparing supper, I produced a fish-hook and line, by the aid of which I soon landed some fine fish, which served admirably to help out the fat pork and corn-bread which would otherwise have been our sole food. Soon after supper I was fast asleep. Long before it was daylight, my slumbers were disturbed by the monotonous tramping of the men on deck, as they poled the boat up against the current; and finding it perfectly impossible to get any more sleep, I turned out of my blanket and plunged head foremost into the creek. After the refreshing *header,* I dressed, and, lighting my pipe, quietly took a seat in the bow of the boat, watching the labours of the men to kill time till breakfast would be ready.

Several times I had heard distant noises to which I paid little heed, not being accustomed to the gobbling of the wild turkey; but at length one, who could not have been more than three hundred yards from the boat, gave a loud gobble, and then there could be no doubt in the mind of anyone who had ever heard the domestic bird of the farm-yard.

"Kome meestair," said the German skipper, tapping me upon the shoulder, "you go see if you can no get for our breakfast a fine turkey."

As the boat was pushed across towards the shore for me to land, an American boy on board said—"You may catch sight of the bird, but I guess you won't kill it; they are about the shyest birds out."

Being a young man, and having a tolerable gun, of course I held a different opinion, though I said nothing. On stepping ashore, I paused a few seconds, hoping to hear the sound repeated, so that I should know in which direction to seek my game; and very shortly the loud notes were again rolled forth. As near as I could judge the sounds seemed to be about three hundred yards off in the forest; so off I started very cautiously, sometimes crawling on hands and knees, taking advantage of every bunch of briar bushes or tree trunk that stood in my path, and

walking as noiselessly as possible. The bird seemed to be very quiet, and I feared that he had taken alarm; but by the time I had worked my way seventy or eighty yards into the forest the gobble was repeated.

Though there was an undergrowth of blackberry bushes, poison vines, and other small plants, the forest was tolerably open. The trees stood at some distance from each other, though their branches interlaced and mingled in such a manner as to check completely the growth of saplings and large bushes; in fact, it was so open that a deer standing up might have been seen at a distance of three to four hundred yards.

Of course the open nature of the ground was against me; so after a few minutes' thought I hid myself behind the trunk of a fallen tree, and there waited till the turkey should give me further information as to his whereabouts. In a few moments the bird again sounded his challenge, and directly afterwards I set eyes for the first time on a wild turkey.

It stood with its head in a listening attitude, one foot slightly raised, as though ready for instant flight; and I at once mentally acknowledged that it was the handsomest bird I had ever seen. In watching his actions, I observed that, although the wings were lowered till they swept the ground and the tail was extended like a huge fan while the fine fellow was in the act of gobbling, yet the moment the sound ceased the wings were folded, the tail was lowered, and every feather was in its place.

As I had only a double-shot gun, fourteen gauge, I felt that my chance of becoming more intimately acquainted with him was very small, inasmuch as the bird stood with its head raised high up, and was at least two hundred yards from the spot where I stood. However, as he seemed disinclined to come towards me, I began to crawl onwards on hands and knees, hoping to be able to reach the spot without disturbing him. My hopes were doomed to be disappointed, for on reaching the spot where he had stood I could no longer see him. Full of disappointment I shouldered my gun, returned to the banks of the creek, overtook the boat, and breakfasted with great disrelish on cold pork, while visions of deviled drumsticks floated before my eyes.

It was about noon when the boat reached the woodyard, and being rather anxious to shine in the eyes of my fellow-voyagers, I again took my gun and strolled out into the woods. I had scarcely gone a hundred yards to the rear of the woodman's shanty, when a fine hen turkey ran from a corn-field into the forest, across a rough road, along which the cord-wood was hauled to the landing-place. To my unpractised eye it appeared so much like a tame bird rambling in the wood that I was afraid to shoot lest I might be called to account for the destruction of farm-yard poultry. But, as some misgivings crossed my mind, I returned to the wood-yard, and inquired if turkeys were kept there?

"Certainly not," was the reply. "The one you saw was a wild bird"; and then followed a peal of laughter at the expense of the greenhorn who had allowed such a prize to escape.

My reputation would have suffered much from this in after years, but being comparatively a stranger in the land, no one expected great deeds from me. I returned to the spot where I had seen the bird, with the idea that it might again cross to the maize field, as it had not been shot at nor very greatly alarmed. I waited about in the road for an hour or two without seeing or hearing anything of it. Just as I was about to return home, I heard a slight noise, and the next instant the turkey again started to cross the road, only accomplishing half the journey, however, for a charge of shot stopped its progress; and I secured my prize and started for the boat, much pleased at having made up for my former lack of success.

Besides man and his deadly fire-arms, the turkeys have other foes; so numerous are its enemies that it seems almost incredible that there should be such numbers still remaining in the forests. Besides the lynx, fox, 'possum, and the varieties of the cat tribe, the turkey has to defend herself and brood against the attacks of birds of prey. Crows and ravens will suck the eggs whenever they have a chance, while the snowy and the Virginian owls seize every opportunity to pounce upon the chicks, or even upon the old birds. Yet it is strange, that while on moonlight nights they will allow the hunter to shoot them one by one, without exhibiting any alarm at the report of his rifle, the appearance of an owl will scare them all from their roosts.

Excepting in Texas, and one or two other States in the South, turkeys are now very shy, from having been so much hunted. The moment they observe a man, they instinctively move from him: they must therefore be approached with much caution. A friend of mine has described the movements and artifices of a celebrated turkey hunter when in pursuit of some veteran gobbler. The quick ear of the hunter having informed him whereabouts his game is, he quickly ensconces himself in ambush, placing a few green bushes before him to hide the muzzle of his rifle. Thus prepared, he takes his call, and gives one solitary *"cluck,"* so exquisitely that it chimes in with the running brook and the rustling leaf. It may be that half a mile off, if the place be favourable for conveying sound, a gobbler is feeding; prompted by his nature, as he scratches up the herbage that conceals his food, he gives utterance to the sounds that first attracted the hunter's attention.

Poor bird! he is bent upon filling his crop; his feelings are listless, commonplace; his wings are awry, the plumage on his breast seems soiled with rain, his wattles are contracted and pale. Look! he starts; every feather instantly assumes its place; he raises his head from the ground and listens: what an eye! what a stride is suggested by that uplifted foot! Gradually the head sinks; again the bright plumage grows dim, and with a low *cluck* he resumes his search for food. The choicest treasures of the American forest are before him; the peccari nut is neglected for an immense grubworm that rolls down a decayed stump, too large to crawl; now a grasshopper is caught; and presently a large ant-hill presents itself, over which the bird leans with wondrous curiosity, peering down the tiny holes out of which the industrious insects are issuing.

Again that *cluck* greets his ear; up rises the head with lightning swiftness, the bird starts forward a pace or two, looks round wonderingly, and then answers back.

No sound is heard but the falling acorn; and it fairly rattles as it dashes from limb to limb, and then falls to the ground. The bird is uneasy; he pecks pettishly, smooths down his feathers, elevates his head slowly, and then brings it to the earth; he raises his wings as if for flight, jumps upon the limb of a fallen tree, looks about, settles down finally into a brown study, and evidently begins to think.

An hour may have passed: he has turned the matter over; his imagination has become inflamed; he has heard just enough to wish to hear more. He is satisfied that no turkey hunter uttered the sounds that reached his ear, for they were too few and far between; and then there rises up in his mind the idea of some disconsolate mistress; and he gallantly flies down from his low perch, gives his body a swaggering motion, and utters a distinct and prolonged *cluck,* significant of both surprise and joy. At that instant the dead twigs near by crack beneath a heavy tread, and off starts the bird, under the impression that he is caught; but the meanderings of some ruminating old cow inform him of his mistake. Composing himself, he listens, until a low *cluck* in the distance reaches his ear.

Now, our gobbler is an old bird, not to be caught with chaff, and several times he has, as if by a miracle, escaped from harm with his life; he has grown very cunning indeed. He will not roost two successive nights upon the same tree, so that daylight never exposes him to the eye of the hunter, who has hidden away in the night with the intention of killing him in the morning's dawn. He never gobbles without running at least a short distance afterwards, as if he were ashamed of the noise he makes; he looks on everything as full of danger, and his experience during his life has heightened the instinct. Twice when young he was coaxed within gunshot, but thanks to some imperfection in the manufacture of the percussion caps, he managed to escape clear. After that, some idle schoolboy, who practised a species of ventriloquism, fooled him, and he would have been slain, had not the urchin, in his anxiety to kill him, overloaded his gun. Three times did he very nearly meet with death by heedlessly wandering along with his thoughtless playfellows. Once he was caught in a pen, but escaped through an overlooked hole in the top; and three feathers of last year's fan decayed beneath the weight of a spring trap.

All this experience has rendered him a very deep bird, and he will sit on a stump pluming himself when common hunters are charming away, but never so wisely as to deceive him twice. They all reveal themselves and their crafty designs by overstepping the modesty of nature: they woo him too much; his loves are far more coy, far less intrusive.

Poor bird! He does not know that the hunter is spreading his snare for him, and is even then so sure of his victim, as to be revolving in his mind whether his goodly carcase shall be a present to a newly married friend, or be served up in savoury fumes upon his own bachelor but hospitable board.

The last *cluck* heard by the gobbler fairly roused him, and he presses

forward; at one time he runs with speed, then stops, as if not yet quite satisfied; something holds him back; still he lingers only for a moment in his course, until coming to a running stream where he will have to fly; the exertion seems too much for him.

Parading with stately strut in the full sunshine, he walks along the margin of the clear water, admiring his fine figure reflected in the sylvan mirror; and then, like some vain lover, tosses his head, as if to say, "Let them come to me." The listless gait is resumed, denoting that for the present the chase is given up.

Gaining the ascent of a low bank that lines the stream which he has just deserted, he stops at the foot of a young beech; in the green moss that fills the interstices of the otherwise smooth bark is hidden away a cricket; the turkey pecks at it without catching it—something annoys him. Like the tiny slipper of Cinderella to the imagination of a young prince, or the glimpses of a waving ringlet or jewelled hand to the glowing passions of a warm, youthful heart, is the remembrance of that sound that now full two hours ago was first heard by our hero, and has in that long time been but twice repeated.

He speculates that in the shady woods surrounding him there must wander a mate; she plucks her food solitarily and calls for him. The monster man, impatient to kill his prey, doles not out his music so softly or so daintily; he fancies that he is not deceived, and that by giving away to his ungallant fears she will be won by another.

"Cluck!"

How well timed was that call! The brave gobbler, now entirely off his guard, contracts himself, opens wide his mouth, and rolls forth fearlessly a volume of sound for his answer.

The stream is crossed in a flutter; the toes scarcely indent themselves in the soft ground over which they pass. On he plunges, until caution again brings him to a halt. We might almost hope that so fine a bird might escape, that there might be given one call too many—one that would grate harshly and unnaturally upon his fine ear. But not so; they lead him onwards to his doom, filling his heart alternately with fear and love.

Again he rolls forth a loud response and listens—yet no answer; his progress is still slow.

The *cluck* again greets his ear; there was a slight quaver attached to it this time, like the forming of a second note. He is nearing the object of his pursuit, and with a loud energetic call he rushes hastily forward, his long neck stretched out and his head moving in a suspicious, though inquiring manner, from side to side.

No longer going round the fallen trees, bushes, and various obstacles in his path but flying over them in love's impetuous haste, he comes at length to an open space, and there stops.

Some six hundred yards from where the noble bird stands may be seen a fallen tree. You can observe some green brush that looks as if it grew out of the decayed wood. In the midst of this innocent-looking brush is hidden away the deadly fowling-piece of the turkey-hunter, and its muzzle is protruding towards the open ground.

Behind it is the hunter himself, lying flat on his stomach on the ground, yet in such a position that the weapon is at his shoulder. He seems to be as dead and motionless as the tree in front of him; and could you watch him closely, you would perceive that he scarcely winks, for fear of alarming the wild and beautiful game.

The turkey still in his exposed situation gobbles; and on the instant the hunter raises his call to his lips, and gives a prolonged *cluck,* loud and shrill—the first that could be construed by the turkey into a direct or positive answer.

The noble bird, now feeling certain of success, fairly dances with delight; he starts forward, his feathers and neck amorously playing as he advances. Now he commences his "strut": his body swells; the beautiful plumage of his breast unfolds itself; his neck curves, drawing the head downward; the wattles assume a scarlet hue, while the skin that covers the head changes like rainbow tints; the long feathers of the wing brush the ground; the tail rises and opens out into a splendid semicircle, while the gorgeously-coloured head becomes beautifully relieved in its centre.

On he comes with a hitching gait, glowing in the sunshine with purple and gold.

The siren *cluck* is twice repeated; he contracts his form to its very smallest dimensions; upwards rises the dainty head to its greatest height; he stands upon his very toes, and looks round suspiciously. Fifty yards of distance protect him from the deadly weapon of the cautious hunter, and with assumed carelessness he even condescends to pick insects from the grass in the open space.

What a trial for the expectant hunter! How vividly does it recur to his mind that even a loud breath has often spoiled a morning's work. The minutes wear on, and then the bird again becomes the caller. He gobbles, opens his form, and, when he is fully bloomed out, the enchanting *cluck* greets his ear. On he comes, like the war-horse, towards the inspiring music of the drum, or like a bark beating against the wind, gallantly but slowly. The dark cold barrel of the gun is not now more silent than the hunter; the game is playing just outside the very edge of its deadly reach—the least mistake and it is gone. One gentle zephyr—one falling twig—might break the charm, and make nature revolt at the shyness apparent in the mistress; and then the gallant lover would wing his way to the woods.

But on he comes. So still is everything, that you can hear his wings distinctly as they brush along the ground; the sun plays in conflicting rays and coloured lights about his gaudily-bronzed plumage. The hunter's finger presses the trigger!—but the time has not yet come.

Suddenly the woods ring in echoing circles back upon the form of the hunter; a sharp report is heard! Out starts, in alarm at the unexpected noise, a blue jay, which squalls as he passes in waving lines before you, so suddenly and unexpectedly was he awakened from his sound sleep. But our rare and beautiful bird—our gallant and noble bird—our cunning and game bird, what has become of him?

The glittering tints have faded from his bright plumage—the gay step has ceased—the bright eye has closed—all are gone. Without a movement of the muscles our valorous lover has fallen lifeless to the earth.

Such is the manner in which the cautious hunter captures a veteran gobbler, one who is used to all the tricks of the woodman's art—one whose wattles have already been cut with shot—one who, though suffering from starvation, would walk by the treasures of grain in the trap and pen—a gobbler who will listen to the plaintive voice of the female till he has tried its quavers, its length, and its repetitions, by every rule which nature has given him, and even then perhaps not answer, except in a smothered voice, for fear of being deceived;—such is the bird which the professed turkey-stalker of Texas will select to break a lance with, and, in spite of the chances against him, will, nine times out of ten, kill.

Here, then, we have the best specimen of the wild forest sports—a trial of skill between the perfection of animal instinct, and the superior mental endowments of man.

In the spring, after I landed at Galveston, I myself paid a visit to a celebrated turkey-hunter; and under his tuition I soon learned more of the habits of the bird, finding that it was more wary and more difficult to take than I had any idea of when I first tried my luck in the woods of Cedar Bayou.

"You will find," said the hunter, while we were projecting a hunt, "that the turkey is of all birds the most crafty game it will ever be your fortune to hunt. It is quite as suspicious as a thief, when he knows that the detective is on his track; the rustling of a dead leaf is sufficient to make it take wing, and so spoil your day's sport. It will start with fright at its own shadow, and run far away from the echoes of its own cry. Its ears are so sharp that I have frequently lost a whole morning's patient stalking when some nimble squirrel has leaped from one branch to another, and broken a dead twig in its haste. And then, too, it has the keenest sight in the world; an eagle is near-sighted compared with the turkey, whose vision can instantly detect any unwonted movement in the bushes, or the flight of a bird of prey as it soars far beyond reach of our eyes. You may approach a bear without the animal becoming aware of your presence, while a deer or hare will generally pause a moment to gaze before it darts away; but with the turkey it is different. To see an enemy is to fly instantly far beyond the reach of danger; and they have a keen instinct which teaches them at once to distinguish enemies from friends or neutrals."

The hunting gear with which my friend exercised his peculiar pastime was simple, though sufficient, consisting of his rifle and his "*caller*"—the musical instrument being constructed from the smaller of the two bones in the middle joint of a hen turkey's wing. So skilled was he in its use, that he was sometimes heard to boast that he "could beat a turkey at talking his own language," and I myself can bear witness that, during the time I sojourned with him, he never failed to kill turkeys whenever he went out into the forest with that intention.

The morning after my arrival at his house we were both on our way to the forest, where he had promised to show me how to call up a turkey. From the general tenor of his conversation it seemed that, although he had killed them early in the autumn, when they were not full grown, as well as in later months, when he hunted them with his trained turkey dogs, yet the sport most to his taste, and, in his opinion, the only legitimate style of turkey-killing, was to call up some crafty old gobbler and fool him.

"It does me good," said he, "to call up a cute old chap that's up to every dodge;—that's the sort I like to have to deal with; and I'll bet a Spanish mule to a rotten pumpkin I drill a hole through him with a rifle bullet before I have done with him."

I took my shot gun with me on this occasion, as my friend had promised to have a cock bird within range if I would attend to his instructions, and keep perfectly quiet. We were on our way to the hunting-grounds before the sun had fairly risen; on the grass and bushes hung a thick dew, which gave promise of a fine bright morning for the sport. The wind was blowing gently towards the north, and we pursued a westerly course, walking to our work right across the wind. When we had gone about a mile and a half, a gobble was plainly heard to our left, and we at once stopped to listen; in the course of five seconds a rival cock answered the challenge.

Having thus satisfied himself that the turkeys were in the neighbourhood, my friend D——, the turkey-hunter, looked about for a place of concealment, and soon found a fallen tree, behind which we sat down, having our guns cocked and in readiness. The tree concealed us perfectly.

Having thus arranged our ambuscade, D—— took his turkey-caller from his bullet-pouch, gave two clear distinct calls, and then listened most eagerly.

The bird we first heard was the first to answer, the wind blowing the sound almost directly towards him; and about two seconds afterwards the one in advance of us answered with three or four gobbles in rapid succession.

"I fear we shall be obliged to let one of them go," whispered D——; "the report of our gun will send the other chap flying in half a second. However, don't fancy we are to have no sport, for the morning is young yet, and we can try our luck elsewhere. But, mark, I shall not answer them for ten minutes; the delay will make them both more anxious."

So excited was I, that the ten minutes seemed at least an hour, but at length D—— gave another call; giving only two *clucks* this time. In an instant the answer from the left-hand bird rolled back on the morning breeze, and a moment afterwards we heard the gobble of the second. It was evident that he, too, had heard the *clucks,* and had answered them rather than his rival; no doubt feeling much more inclined to make love than to declare war.

"That sounds more healthy," exclaimed D——; "after all we stand a chance of killing the pair."

From the voices of the two birds, their gobbling sounding much nearer than when first heard, it was evident that they were approaching us at a rapid rate, and I felt rather surprised that D—— did not repeat the sounds which lured them so far.

"I shall leave them alone for a few minutes," said he, reading my thoughts; "It is quite probable that they have already had a battle for the good graces of some plump hen, and so they will make a race of it to see who can get to her first."

At least a quarter of an hour passed by, during which the turkey-hunter remained as motionless and quiet as the old tree-stump which concealed him. The two cocks, however, were not so cautious; and at frequent intervals they rolled out loud sonorous gobbles, both as challenges to each other, and to elicit a response from the unseen seeming hen. D—— was almost as excited as myself, though being more accustomed to this kind of still-hunting, his agitation was not so apparent. He made not the least noise; conveying his ideas to me as he was able by means of signs.

"They'll meet together presently," he signalled with his lip, "and then I can call them both up."

To the rivals the hen bird must have seemed excessively shy and coy, for no enticing *cluck* encouraged their advances, while they filled the air with invitations and declarations of love and war. As minute after minute passed away, the birds seemed to become more and more excited.

"It is all right now," D—— at length whispered, putting his mouth close to my ear. "They'll come close to us as soon as I give another *cluck;* so get your gun ready to follow my shot. I'll take the right-hand bird and shoot first, because you can work your shot gun quicker than I can the rifle."

So saying, D—— glanced at his weapon, to see that all was right, and then again sent forth two clear, distinct calls from the little bone between his lips. This done, he at once dropped the instrument which had done such wonders into his bullet-pouch, and grasping his rifle, prepared to fire—kneeling on one knee, and resting his elbow on the other.

As he had told me, it was indeed a race between the noble birds. All their native caution seemed thrown aside, and they came running with eager haste till they were not more than thirty paces from the log that sheltered us. Then, not seeing the expected hen, they paused, as though to discover her whereabouts. They brushed their wings along the ground, and extended their fans; the skins of their necks and heads assumed as many tints as a rainbow or soap-bubble, as they experienced alternately the passions of love and anger. In loud notes they defied each other, and sought to obtain a response of admiration from the hen, who, they felt certain, was hidden in the wood close by, doubtless looking with admiring eyes on their splendid plumage and gallant behaviour.

Suddenly was heard the sharp crack of a rifle, and the woods around rang in a thousand echoing circles, while a light cloud of white smoke floated gently upwards, seeming at length to become entangled in the branches of the trees overhead.

One splendid bird lay upon the mossy ground, his head cleft by the unerring bullet; while the rival, after standing one half second in seeming bewilderment, made a movement as though to take flight. But even that slight hesitation was sufficient to enable me to cover him with my gun, and then half a dozen buckshot stretched him dead, although not so cleanly killed as had been his brother in misfortune. D—— rose to his feet and reloaded his rifle, while I renewed the charge in the right barrel of my gun.

"We have them both," he said, "just as I expected. But I hope you paid particular attention to my calling."

"Yes. I thought it was the best imitation of a hen turkey I had ever heard. Had I not seen the call in your mouth, I should have fallen into the same mistake that cost these beauties their lives."

"That is not what I mean. Did you notice how very little I called, and what long intervals I allowed between each *cluck?*"

"Certainly," I replied.

The old hunter filled his pipe, and was enveloped in a cloud of smoke, before he went on.

"Then just remember that, if you wish to have much sport in wild turkey calling, you may pipe as little as you please, so long as the cock answers your summons. I find that many fools from the old settlements, who fancy themselves hunters, will pipe away, as if for the pleasure of hearing their own noise; but you should remember that a gobbler has a good ear for music, and will in an instant detect a false or unnatural note; and this, too, any gobbler who has reached years of discretion would be much more likely to run *from* than *to* such an infernal hubbub. Depend upon it, more turkeys are lost in that way than by calling too little. But come along to breakfast."

After this I frequently amused myself in the woods on fine spring mornings by calling up gobblers, and always found my friend correct in his opinions and instructions.

But there is another kind of sport better suited to the winter months before the gobblers would answer a call: and that is, hunting them with a properly trained turkey dog. A well-trained dog will never range very far from his master till he finds the warm scent of a single turkey or a flock. Then he will start upon the trail without giving tongue until he finds the game. He will then run on, and by continual yelping, compel it to ascend some tree. If it is a single bird, he will then sit beneath the branch where the turkey has taken refuge, and continue to bark till his master arrives, and with a well-directed shot brings the bird to the ground.

In this kind of hunting, the more the dog barks when he has "treed" the game, the greater is the hunter's chance of success, because by so doing it distracts the bird's attention, and the hunter is often able to approach unobserved. For two reasons, the hunter should approach and shoot behind the bird: in the first place, the turkey, in all probability, will not see him, being too much engaged in watching the motions of the dog; and, in the second place, the closely set feathers will turn aside even small-sized buckshot if aimed at the breast; it is, therefore, much the wiser plan to shoot up the feathers than against them. I soon found that the latter method did not pay, having in my early days of gobbler-hunting lost many a fine bird by vainly expending a charge of shot against the bird's armour-plated breast.

In approaching the treed bird, so as to get a shot, the hunter must exercise much patience and caution, as the bird invariably takes wing and is lost if it discovers the least sign of a human being. Its instinct tells it that in the tree it has nothing to fear from the dog. A single bird is much more easily killed than one in a flock, because in the latter case so many keen bright eyes are prying about, that some individual of the gang is almost sure to see the hunter, and then the slightest movement causes them to take flight, while a single bird is occupied in watching the dog.

During my stay with my friend D——, whose prowess and cunning have been already described, and who taught me to call up cocks, we used to cross the river from Washington County, where his settlement was, and hunt in the Brazos County twice or thrice a week. As an average, the proceeds of our day's sport would be a couple of deer, and perhaps eight turkeys, of which I must confess D—— killed the lion's share.

The best season for this kind of sport was, in our opinion, from the middle of October till the end of January, when the male birds begin to seek out their mates, and the season for calling commences. After the 1st of February, we very rarely shot at a hen-turkey till the following autumn, when she had reared her brood.

At the time I speak of, Brazos County, although a large tract of land, had no more inhabitants than a little country village, and was almost entirely covered with forest. This was a dozen years ago; and although, no doubt, some clearings have been made, there is still enough of the ancient woods left to harbour swarms of game. When I was there my friend D—— called the place his poultry-yard—so large was the quantity of turkeys which he killed there.

Sometimes turkey roosts are discovered by the hunter, who will mark the spot well, and then return at night when the moon is full. At such times the birds seem stupefied, and a tolerable marksman will have a good chance of killing half the flock; although if a wild cat appeared on the tree, or an owl sailed over head, all their instinct of self-preservation would return.

I have casually spoken of trapping turkeys; but as no thorough sportsman can feel anything but disgust at such a method of killing game, I shall not enlarge on the subject. With his good gun, a well-trained dog, and the instructions of a veteran woodsman, more and nobler sport can be obtained, and the young hunter can eat the game that falls to his gun, without feeling that he has killed a bird in a manner which is considered unfair both here and in America.

Turkeys can be killed wholesale by destroying the hen when her chicks are half-grown, and then calling up the brood; but this is rarely done by the backwoods' hunters although they are not restricted as to the quantity they may kill, nor the time at which it is lawful to kill. But this I know, that the man who would kill a doe in fawn, except accidentally, or would destroy turkeys in the last-mentioned manner, would be looked upon with as much dislike by American hunters as he would by English game-preservers.

By my last received accounts, game is more plentiful than ever on the Texan prairies; and, doubtless, many English sportsmen will be tempted across the Atlantic. For myself, I can only say—"Would I were there!"*

---

* Captain Flack, *A Hunter's Experiences in the Southern States of America*, London, 1866, pp. 232–258.

The Virginian Canaan

DAVID H. STROTHER

David Hunter Strother (1816–1888) was a Virginian of the old school, though Martinsburg, his birthplace and home, became a part of West Virginia when the state was split off in 1863, and he served during the Civil War as a brigadier general in the Union army. His claim to fame rests on a batch of descriptive articles and travel sketches on his native state, on North Carolina, and other areas, contributed chiefly to *Harper's Magazine.* As well received as his articles were the numerous pen-and-ink drawings which he also provided as illustrations. His nom de plume, "Porte Crayon," was thus peculiarly appropriate.

The selection, "The Virginian Canaan" (accent on the second *a*), started him off on his career as a *Harper's* contributor with a graphic account of a gentleman's expedition into the Blackwater Falls wilderness. In the 1850's this area was still a virgin jungle of mountain laurel and rhododendron thickets so dense that even the Indians had avoided it for fear of being lost, and the pioneer trails leading to the West had given it a wide berth. Its scenic beauties are to this day of the first order, and the Blackwater Falls State Park presently established on a tiny portion of the immense tract provides one of the most beautiful mountain retreats in the Appalachians. In 1852, the year of Strother's junket, the Canaan Valley was a paradise for the fisherman and the hunter; and while its forests are now principally second-growth, it continues to rank high in the esteem of West Virginia's sportsmen.

Strother's humor, his picturesque details, and his pen sketches— all combined to make his description of the Blackwater expedition such a success with both readers and editors that *Harper's* soon commissioned a whole series on "Virginia Illustrated." After serialization, these articles were brought out in 1857 as a book with the same title, and a second edition followed in 1871. In the past few years his work has been rediscovered, and further material from his pen has been rounded up in book form; in 1960

Cecil D. Eby, Jr., provided an excellent biography, *"Porte Crayon": The Life of David Hunter Strother.*

Like William Elliott and Captain Flack, Strother makes the windlass creak in pulling in "literary" touches, but he also exhibits a sharp eye for homely detail and a zest for honestly reporting aspects of the backwoods that often seemed too trivial to warrant the notice of an age fonder of the high-falutin than our own.

IN Randolph County, Virginia, is a tract of country containing from seven to nine hundred square miles, entirely uninhabited, and so savage and inaccessible that it has rarely been penetrated even by the most adventurous. The settlers on its borders speak of it with a sort of dread, and regard it as an ill-omened region, filled with bears, panthers, impassable laurel-brakes, and dangerous precipices. Stories are told of hunters having ventured too far, becoming entangled, and perishing in its intricate labyrinths. The desire of daring the unknown dangers of this mysterious region stimulated a party of gentlemen, who were at Towers' Mountain House on a trouting excursion, to undertake it, in June, 1851. They did actually penetrate the country as far as the Falls of the Blackwater, and returned with marvelous accounts of its savage grandeur, and the quantities of game and fish to be found there. One of the party wrote an entertaining narrative of their adventures and sufferings, which was published in a stout volume*—which every body ought to read.

During the winter of 1852, several of the same party, with other friends, planned a second trip, to be undertaken on the first of June following. At that date, so fully was the public mind occupied with filibustering and President-making, that the notes of preparation for this important expedition were scarcely heard beyond the corporate limits of the little town of M———, in the Valley of Virginia. Even in this contracted circle the excitement was principally confined to the planners themselves, while the public looked on with an apathy and unconcern altogether unaccountable. Indeed, some narrow-minded persons went so

---

* [Pendleton Kennedy,] *The Blackwater Chronicle, A Narrative of an Expedition into the Land of Canaan . . . ,* New York, 1853.

far as to say, that it was nothing but a scheme of idleness to waste time; and advised the young gentlemen to stick to their professions, and let the bears alone. But, as may be supposed, all such met the usual fate of gratuitous counselors who advise people against their inclinations.

In the daily meetings which were held for five months previous to the date fixed for their departure, our adventurers discussed freely and at great length every thing that appertained, or that could in any way appertain, to the subject in view, from the elevation of the mountains and the course of rivers, down to the quality of a percussion cap and the bend of a fish-hook. They became students of maps and geological reports; read Izaak Walton's "Complete Angler" and "Le Guide et Hygiène des Chasseurs"; consulted Count Rumford and Doctor Kitchener, and experimented largely in the different kinds of aliments most proper for the sustenance of the human system. Mr. Penn, the author, copied at length a recipe for making cat-fish soup, assuring his friends that when surfeited with venison and trout, this dish would afford them a delightful change. Mr. Porte Crayon, the artist, also furnished frequent designs for hunting-coats, caps, knapsacks, and leggings, modeled, for the most part, from those of the French army in Algiers. "For," said he, "the French are the most scientific people in the world; and as they have paid more attention to the equipment of their army than any other, everything they adopt is presumed to be perfect of its kind."

The result of all this studying and talking was, that every one differed from his friend, and equipped himself after his own fashion; and the commissary department suddenly concluded that biscuit and bacon were the most substantial, portable, and palatable articles of food known to the dwellers south of the Potomac, and accordingly made arrangements to have ample supplies of both ready for the occasion.

With the opening spring the buds began to swell and the blue-birds to warble, and the zeal of our adventurers kept pace with the season, so that by the first of April all were ready, fully equipped, "straining like grayhounds in the slip." The intolerable vacuum between this and the starting day might be graphically illustrated by leaving half a dozen blank pages; but as such a procedure might be misunderstood, or characterized as clap-trap, it may be preferable to fill up the blank by introducing the *dramatis personae* who are to figure in the following narrative:

Mr. Penn, an author of some distinction, has already been mentioned. He is gaunt and tall, with distinguished air and manners, flowing and graceful gestures, prominent and expressive eye, indicating, according to Phrenology, a great command of language. In this case, however, the science was at fault, for when Mr. Penn got fairly started in discourse he had no command over his language at all. It poured forth in an irresistible torrent, carrying away the speaker himself, and overwhelming or putting to flight his audience.

Mr. Dindon, a fine, athletic sportsman, not a dandiacal popper at quails and hares, but a real Nimrod, a slayer of wild turkeys and deer, to whom the excitement of the chase was as the breath of his nostrils; and who sometimes forgot even that in his keen appreciation of the poetry of forest life. He was never known either to be wearied in a hunt or silenced in a debate.

Mr. Jones was somewhat inclined to be stout, not to say fat. Mr. J. was equally fond of rural sports and personal comforts. Ambitious of being considered a thoroughgoing sportsman, he kept the best dog and the most beautiful gun in the district. He frequently appeared covered with his hunting accoutrements, followed by his dog, and generally went out alone. Prying persons remarked that his game-bag was usually fuller when he went out than when he returned. Dindon, who was knowing in these matters, always said that Mr. J. was a humbug; and all this apparent fondness for the chase was a sham; that Jones, as soon as he got out of sight of town, found some shady place, ate the dinner that stuffed the game-bag, and went to sleep; when he woke, would drag himself through a thicket hard by, muddy his boots in a swamp, and return with the marks of severe fatigue and determined hunting upon him, and with whatever game he might be able to purchase from straggling urchins or old negroes who had been lucky with their traps. For the rest, Mr. Jones had some rare companionable qualities. He could give a joke with enviable point and readiness, and take one with like grace and good-humor.

The sprightly sketches which illuminate this unskillful narrative are the most appropriate and shall be the only introduction of our friend PORTE CRAYON. He has rendered the subjects with great truthfulness, and has exhibited even some tenderness in the handling of them. If he has nothing extenuated, he has, at least, set down naught in malice. Porte, indeed, modestly remarks that his poor abilities were entirely inadequate to do justice either to the sublimity of the natural scenery or the preposterous absurdity of the human species on that memorable expedition.

Mr. Smith, a gentleman of imposing presence, of few words, but an ardent and determined sportsman, and zealous promoter of the expedition, completes the catalogue.

Sometime during the month of May, X. M. C. (for certain reasons his initials only are used), an accomplished and talented gentleman residing at a distance from M——, received a letter which ran as follows:

"Dear X.—We have fixed upon the 1st of June to start for the Canaan Country. Our party will consist of Dindon, Jones, Smith, your old friend Penn, and myself. Can you join us? If so, give us immediate notice, and set about making your preparations without delay. I would recommend to you to procure the following equipment: a waterproof knapsack, fishing tackle, and a gun; a belt with pistols—a revolver would be preferable, in case of a conflict with a panther; a hunting-knife for general purposes—a good ten-inch blade, sharp and reliable. It will be useful for cleaning fish, dressing game, and may serve you a turn when a bear gets you down in a laurel-brake. Store your knapsack with an extra pair of shoes, a change of raiment, such as will resist water and dirt to the last extremity, a pair of leggings to guard against rattlesnakes, and the following eatables: one dozen biscuit, one pound of ham, one pound of ground coffee, salt, pepper and condiments. This will be the private store of each person, the public supplies will be carried out on horses.

"The place of rendezvous is the Berkeley Springs, the day the 31st of May.

"Yours in haste,
PORTE CRAYON."

The Correspondence Committee had the gratification of receiving a favorable reply to the foregoing: "Mr. X. will certainly come." All right; the party is made up. The last of May has come. Mr. Crayon, in full hunting costume, is standing on the portico of the great hotel at the Berkeley Springs. Messrs. Jones and Smith have arrived; their equipments have been examined and pronounced unexceptionable. Here comes X. What a pair of leggings! and there's Penn with him, in a blue blouse out at the elbows, with a rod like Don Quixote's lance.

"Ah, gentlemen! well met," shouted Penn, as they approached.

"You see before you a personification of Prince Hal, at a time when he kept rather low company," quoth Mr. Jones; "he looks more like Poins on a thieving expedition."

"Ah! my fat friend, are you there? glad to see you. I have a rod here, gentlemen, that will make you envious. See how superbly balanced; what a spring it has! the very thing for brook-fishing, for whipping the smaller streams. And then see how easily carried." And, suiting the action to the word, he unjointed it, and slipped it into a neat case, portable, light, and elegant. "I procured one of the same sort for Smith when I was in New York. I will show you also a supply of artificial flies," continued Mr. Penn, drawing a leather case from his knapsack, "and a fine bug calculated for the largest sized trout."

Here he produced a bug, which renewed the astonishment and hilarity of the company.

"What is it for?" "What sort of creature is it?" "What does it represent?" shouted one and all.

"I have not dipped into entomology lately, but I have been assured that this bug is calculated to take none but the largest fish. No small fish will approach it, from personal apprehension; and no trout under twenty-two inches in length would venture to swallow it."

"If I were called upon to classify that bug," said Mr. Jones, "I would call it a *Chimera*—in the vernacular, *Humbug!*"

"Come to supper," said Porte. "We start at two o'clock to-night by the train."

The sun that rose fair and bright on the morning of the first of June found our fishermen just entering the United States Hotel, in the town of Cumberland. "Who the—are they?" inquired one of the matutinal loafers in the barroom.

"Oh! they be some o' these Hungry fellers, I reckon," replied a gaping stable boy.

"Right, boy! right!" said Mr. Jones; "quite right; here's a dime. Landlord, let us have breakfast in the shortest time imaginable."

The route from Cumberland to the Oakland depot, on the summit of the Alleghanies, and the trip from thence by wagon to Towers', was as barren of notable adventure as it was fruitful in jokes and hilarity. At Towers' they found their old comrade, Mr. Dindon, who had gone ahead to procure guides, horses, &c.

"Well! what have you brought up?" asked Dindon.

"Eleven hundred and forty biscuit, twenty pounds of ground coffee, forty pounds of middling and two hams; lard, salt, pepper, sugar, *et cetera*. All well packed and in good order. What have you done?"

"The eight loaves of bread are ready." "Good!"—"The horses are ready." "Good!"—"The guides are still to be looked after." "Hum!—let us see the horses."—"Andrew, bring out the animals."

Lame Kit and Old Sorry here made their first appearance on the stage, and were received with mingled laughter and indignation. Lame Kit's fore-leg was as stiff as a ramrod; and Old Sorry, among other defects, was blind and distempered.

"What an inhuman idea!" said Mr. Jones; "you don't really mean to afflict these wretched tackies with such loads of baggage as we have here."

Mr. Dindon was aroused. "I'll bet a thousand dollars you haven't two such horses on your estate."

"No, I'll swear to it," responded Jones. "If I had, I'd have them shot within an hour."

"No, sir," rejoined Dindon, with heat. "I mean that you can't produce their equals for strength and endurance."

"I won't take advantage of you," said Jones, "but will offer you a more equal bet: That if you load them with this baggage neither of them will live to reach the banks of the Cheat River."

"That shows your judgment in horseflesh; but what can be expected of a man educated north of the Potomac? What can he know about horses?"

Mr. Jones assumed an attitude confronting Mr. Dindon. "I'd like to know," said he, "if Northern horses are not universally conceded to be superior to Southern?"

"Gentlemen," interposed X., "I foresee an interminable wrangle. We'll adjourn—cough them down."

The following day was spent in engaging guides. Thornhill, an intelligent, energetic, good-tempered fellow, agreed to undertake it. His dwelling was a specimen of rural architecture not noticed by Downing, nor characterized by any of the writers on that subject. Porte declared it looked like the connecting link between a hut and a wood-pile. But, like the pearl in the oyster, the gem of disinterested hospitality is found as frequently in these humble abodes as in the proudest mansions of our good old State.

All things being arranged at Towers' for an early start on the third, Crayon and X. M. C. shouldered their guns and knapsacks, and started for Conway's nine miles distant, on the route to the Canaan country. They were to engage Conway to accompany the party, and to be in readiness to join the main body as they passed in the morning. Crayon had traveled the road on a former occasion, and as he pretended to considerable skill in woodcraft, confidently took the lead, and struck into the forest by a blind path. For four or five miles all went well, until the declining sun was hidden by the tall crowns of the firs, and the path became more and more indistinct. Crayon became thoughtful, and dropped behind.

"Whose dogs are these?" quietly asked X.

Crayon looked up, and saw two wolves standing in the path, within thirty paces of them, staring with amazement at the strange intruders. In the twinkling of an eye his piece was leveled, but the wolves, with equal celerity, had betaken themselves to the bushes.

"Well, you don't say they were wolves? I supposed they were some of the neighbor's dogs. What a mortification! I might have shot them both."

"There are no neighbors hereabouts, X., and no dogs wandering about. The rule is to crack away at every four-legged creature you see, and the chances are that it is legitimate game. But we must be moving; night is coming rapidly on. Push on for Conway's."

Within the next mile Mr. Crayon came to a stand-still. "X.," said he, musingly, "at what hour does the moon rise to-night?"

"Don't know—haven't observed—are we not near Conway's?"

"My friend, it is useless to disguise matters; in fifteen minutes it will be pitch-dark. I have seen no trace of a path for the last half mile; this country looks strange to me. I couldn't go back if I would, I wouldn't go if I could; we should be laughed at."

"This life is all new to me," said X., with resignation; "but go on, and I'll follow till death."

"X., can you see a star, or any thing that might serve as a guide, to prevent us from making circles?"

"No, I can see nothing but trees and bushes, and can hardly see them."

"Follow on, then; we'll try it."

As they trudged on, the forest grew murkier and darker, and the undergrowth more dense and tangled.

"Where are you, Porte?" "Here; come on."—"Ho! I'm up to my knees in a marsh!" "Hist! did you hear that?"—"Yes; keep close, and don't shoot, or we may kill each other; be careful of your firearms, and depend on your hunting-knife." "Good Heavens! we are getting into a laurel-brake. Turn back, or we are gone."

On they struggled, torn by briars, throttled by wild vines, and tripped up by fallen timber.

"Porte! stop. I'm ready to perish with fatigue; let us rest a while on this log."

"X., did you ever sleep in the woods?"

"No, I never did."

"Have you anything to eat in your knapsack?"

"Not a mouthful; to lighten my load, I tumbled mine into the general provision-bag."

"I did the same thing."

"How unlucky! I will take this impressive opportunity, Mr. X., to read you a lesson in woodcraft. Never leave the camp without a day's provision with you."

"But are we likely to get to Conway's to-night?"

"The probabilities seem to be against it; but let us try again."

Another hour of fruitless toil, and no hope.

"X., don't it seem to be getting lighter on our left hand?"

"Ho! by all that's jolly I'm on open ground, and feel something like a beaten track under my feet."

A broad gleam of light shot across the wood, like the sudden flash of a torch, revealing a long vista in the forest and the trodden and rutted surface of the highway.

"Whoop! whoop! hurrah!—the moon and the big road—the big road and the moon. I knew it! I knew I couldn't be mistaken. Here's the stream; we're not a mile from Conway's."

The wanderers, notwithstanding their fatigue and knapsacks, indulged in a *pas de deux* and an embrace, and cheerily resumed their route. The moon rose higher and higher; anon they heard the bark of a dog—a long-welcome bow-wow. X. quoted Byron:

" 'Tis sweet to hear the watch dog's honest bark."

Then they came to a clearing with a double cabin in the midst. The chorus of dogs was at its full.

"Get out, ye whelps! Who's there?"

"Hallo! Old Otter, come out of your den. Here are friends."

The old man stuck his weasel face out of the door, and after a short scrutiny, recognized Porte Crayon. "Well done," said he; "but I'm glad to see ye. I heard ye were in the country, but I didn't expect to see ye at this time o' night. But come in, ye must be hungry. Gals, get up, and find the gentlemen some supper."

The old man's buxom daughters tumbled out of a bed in a dark corner of the room, and soon the fresh-heaped fire roared and sparkled in the chimney, and the table was spread with the best in the house— cold bread and meat, fragrant glades butter, rich milk, and maple beer. As they supped, they narrated their adventure with the wolves, at which their host chuckled greatly. A bed in the spare room of the cabin received the weary couple, who slept soundly until the morning. "How delicious! what an invigorating atmosphere! what a magnificent forest is this that walls us round!" were their first exclamations on issuing from the cabin. They breakfasted and took their seats upon a comfortable stump in front of the house while Conway completed his simple arrangements for the journey. "Is the fat gentleman in your company this time?" inquired he. "Well, I never expected to a-seed him agin. Is the big-eyed gentleman coming, too?—he that writ a book, I disremember his name. And the one with spectacles?"

"Yes, they are all coming."

Anon loud voices are heard issuing from the depths of the forest, which gradually approach, until those of Mr. Jones and Mr. Dindon are distinguishable, and the words, confusedly mingled, Northern horses— Southern horses—trotters—thousand dollars—Eclipse—then a long string of expletives. The head of the column emerges from the wood; this is no other than the fat man, stripped to his silk shirt and pantaloons, with a great pack on his back and a sapling in his hand; he was a good personification of Orson of the Wood. He presently halted and faced about.

"Mr. Dindon, I say—hush! you have the advantage of wind in this argument, but not of reason. You know I am short of breath; I can't walk and discuss at the same time; it is ungenerous to press it now—wait until we halt for dinner. At present, I say, peremptorily—hush!"

The detachment from Conway's now joined the march—and, whooping, laughing, singing, and wrangling, they wound along under the gloomy archway of the trackless forest. Thornhill, with his tomahawk belted about him, led the van. Dindon, Crayon, and Penn followed; then came Lame Kit, led by Conway; and Old Sorry, conducted by Powell, a hunter, who was engaged to go in with them to bring the horses out after they had reached their destination. Smith and X. M. C. formed the rear-guard, and far behind lagged Mr. Jones, probably with the intention of avoiding useless discussion, and of managing his wind to the greatest advantage. After a march of six miles, they entered a green glade of great beauty, watered by an amber rivulet, which they leaped with their packs and guns. This rivulet was the infant Potomac; that leap was from Maryland into Virginia. Now they breasted a mountain—a long, tiresome tug it was, that took the conceit out of more than one of the party who started fair that morning. On the summit they took a breathing spell. This is the dividing-ridge between the waters of the East and the West. In a short time they crossed another amber brook, a tributary of the Ohio, and one of the immediate sources of the Blackwater. About five o'clock in the afternoon they emerged from the dreary forest into another waving glade, and at the further border Thornhill gave the welcome order to halt for the night. Cheerfully our adventurers deposited their guns and knapsacks; and after a brief repose, joined the hunters in heaping up dry logs and combustibles for the camp-fire. How the fire blazed and crackled! how grandly the smoke volumed up among the lofty tree-tops! The horses, relieved of their burdens, were tethered in the glade, up to their bellies in grass. While preparations for supper were going on, several of the party got out their fishing-tackle, and tried the little stream that watered the glade. It was alive with trout; and half an hour after, a hundred of the small fry were served up at supper with the biscuit and bacon. It was a meal that a monarch might envy. A good bed of hemlock branches was duly spread, the fire replenished with larger logs; and the weary party disposed itself to sleep as best it might, pillowed on log or knapsack. The excitement produced by the novelty of the situation kept X. awake. The gloom of the forest around was intense; the camp-fire blazed in the centre of a group of four lofty firs, whose straight and mast-like trunks were illuminated by its light for a hundred feet without the interruption of a limb, and whose tops interlaced and formed a lofty and almost impervious covering over the sleepers. X. raised himself upon his elbow, and broke the silence.

"What a picturesque scene! What a couch! What a canopy! What sublime bed-posts!"

"Go to sleep, poet," growled a drowsy fellow, "or you'll be sorry for it to-morrow."

Presently a noise was heard in the forest—a wild, unearthly cry—an incomprehensible sound—everybody sprang up. "What the deuce is it?" inquired the sleepers, rubbing their eyes. "Gentlemen," said Mr. Dindon, deliberately cocking his rifle, "get your arms ready. I know that sound well—it is the cry of a wolf." Again the terrible voice echoed through the wood, nearer and more distinct. There was a general clicking of gun-locks;—Jones, who had made himself a comfortable nest at the foot of a tree, pitched into the centre of the group; Crayon sat the picture of deliberate valor, with hunting-knife in one hand, revolver in the other, and a rifle lying across his lap; X. crept on all fours to get possession of his double-barrel; Penn, in whose poetic bosom the joy of meeting with an adventure over-balanced every personal consideration, with nervous haste drew forth his book, and began noting down the incident;—Thornhill and Powell, however, so far from evincing any anxiety, seemed bursting with suppressed laughter; while Conway sat smoking his pipe with imperturbable gravity. Here is an extract from Mr. Penn's note-book:

"*Camp No. 1—10 o'clock p.m.*—Disturbed by a terrible cry, somewhat resembling this: too-too—too-hoo—too-too—too-hoo. Supposed to be wolves or panthers. In momentary expectation of an attack. If we perish.... *Half-past ten.* Sounds ascertained to proceed from owls of the largest size, but not dangerous. Camp calm, and disposed to slumber."

Next morning our adventurers were stirring betimes—refreshed the half-extinct fire—dispatched a hasty breakfast—and resumed their march before sunrise. This was a hard day for most of them. The broken sleep and unusual beds had not done much to repair the fatigues of the previous day—the hills were steeper, and the fallen timber cumbered the route so greatly that they were frequently obliged to make long *détours* to find a passage practicable for the horses.

The bodies of these fallen giants afforded quite a curious spectacle as they lay prone and supine, singly and in monstrous heaps; frequently, a hundred and fifty feet in length, and eighteen in girth, coated with a rich covering of moss, and their decayed wood affording a soil for thickets of seedlings of their own and other species. Sometimes they were seen spanning a ravine at a giddy height, like suspension-bridges, the parasite growth forming a parapet, or hand-rail, as if for the safety and convenience of the passer. Sometimes the faithless surface yielded to the tread, and the astounded hunter found himself imbedded to the armpits, in what he had supposed to be solid wood. The climbing of these barricades was one of the principal items in the fatigue of the journey, and any one who happened to look back on that day would generally see Mr. Jones astride of one of them, beseeching the party to wait awhile. It would have been well for the venatical reputation of Mr. Jones if the events of this day could be effaced from the record, or covered by a black veil, like the face of Marino Faliero among the Doges of Venice.

"Look at him," quoth Dindon, triumphantly; "he pretended to underrate that lame mare, and now he's glad to hang to her tail. He said she couldn't carry her load to the Cheat River, and now she is carrying his knapsack and himself into the bargain. I suppose, Mr. Jones, you'll now acknowledge you're no judge of horse-flesh."

"It's too bad," said X. "Let go, Jones; have you no greatness of soul? don't you see the poor beast can hardly get along?"

But deaf alike to satire or remonstrance, Mr. Jones kept his hold until Kit, with a long-drawn groan, stood stock still. "Thar now," said the hunter. "I've been a-looking for her to drop." The mare was released, and Jones attempted to seize Old Sorry by the same appendage. He, however, being too blind to see the justice of such a proceeding, relieved himself with a kick.

The hunters had been dodging the laurel-brakes all day. They seemed to dread the passage, and would frequently go miles around to avoid it. They had heard stories of men who had spent days in them, wandering in circles, and who had finally perished from starvation; and they say when once fairly in there is no calculating when you will get out. Some of these brakes extend for many miles, and are so dense that even the deer can not pass except by finding the thinnest places, and when the experienced woodman is forced to cross, he always seeks a deer-path. The ponderous strength of the bear enables him to traverse them more easily. In them he makes his lair, and our adventurers often found the laurel recently torn and broken by bears, in going to and from their places of retreat. With the horses the passage could not even be attempted without a previous clearing of the way by the ax-men. Upon consultation, it was considered necessary to cross the brake before them, and the guides went into it lustily, while the rest of the company, one after another, dropped asleep. In about two hours the way was cleared, but it was with much difficulty that the horses could be induced to proceed. The guides swore like the army in Flanders, Kit's stiff leg would not yield to circumstances, and Sorry became several times so tangled that he had to be released by the ax. The footmen passed ahead of the horses, and soon found themselves in similar circumstances. They sank up to their knees in mud and water; they were throttled by the snake-like branches of the laurel, and were frequently obliged to resort to their hunting-knives to extricate a leg or an arm from its grasp. Ascending the stump of a riven hemlock, a striking picture presented itself. The laurel waved up and down as far as the eye could reach, like a green lake, with either shore walled by the massive forest, and out of its bed, rising singly or in groups of three or four, the tallest and most imposing of the fir species. The heads of our adventurers sometimes appeared hidden as they struggled through—and whether visible or invisible, the crackling of branches, the rustling of leaves, and a rolling fire of execrations marked their progress. All else was silent.

Toward evening a bear was seen, but so worn and spiritless were the adventurers that no one thought of pursuing it. All were anxious to

reach the river that evening, as they had proposed. At length the ridge upon which they traveled seemed suddenly to terminate, and they heard, far below, the rushing of waterfalls. Here they came willingly to a halt, while the guides descended the mountain to ascertain their position. In the course of an hour they returned, reporting that the roaring was from the Falls of the Blackwater, and that they now overlooked the site of the encampment of the last season. By this time it had grown so dark and rained so heavily that it became indispensable to look for a place of encampment. The men dispersed to look for water, taking care, however, always to keep within calling distance of each other. Water was soon found on the border of a laurel-brake, a most cheerless spot for a bivouac. The rain fell in torrents. The horses were unloaded, and a young birch cut down for them to browse upon, in default of grass. While some were trying, apparently without success, to get together dry combustibles for a fire, others endeavored to secure the provisions, arms, and ammunition from the rain; and some sunk down on the spot where they halted, and wrapping their blankets about them, slept in spite of every thing. A more cheerless prospect for a night could scarcely be imagined. With garments soaked, blankets wet, every leaf dripping with water, and the earth covered with moss and dead leaves, like a sponge thoroughly saturated; stiff with fatigue and shivering with cold, there seemed to be little chance of obtaining either rest or fire. Conway's woodcraft, however, triumphed over all difficulties. With knife and hatchet he peeled the bark from a fir about four feet in circumference. With this he sheltered the fire until it got headway, and then heaping on such wood as was the most combustible there was soon a cheerful roaring blaze that defied the rain. He next with forks, props, and cross-poles erected the framework of a shed, twelve or fourteen feet long, which was speedily covered with bark, and afforded a complete shelter. The ground beneath was covered with hemlock branches, shaken and dried over the fire, to serve at once for seats and bedding. Fried middling and hot coffee were then served round, and from a most forlorn and unpromising beginning our adventurers found themselves in comparatively comfortable circumstances. Mr. Jones was as usual an object of peculiar attention. On their arrival at the halting place Mr. Jones observed a large hemlock, which threw out its roots like the arms of a sofa. Between them a plump cushion of moss, which had hitherto escaped the rain, seemed to invite him to a seat. Mr. J. accepted the invitation, and set about making himself as comfortable as possible. Upon examining the ground about him, it occurred that just over his seat would be a very proper place to build the shed, and he gave orders accordingly. Whether from a malicious suggestion of some one else, or some sly waggery of his own, Conway took pains to locate the fire and shed at some distance off. Mr. Jones argued and remonstrated, but to no effect. The savor of supper enticed him from his lair for a short time, and he then found that the shed was so full there was not room for a ramrod. Mr. Jones was not a ramrod, nor was he to be outdone so easily; he took Conway aside in a mysterious manner, and whispered something in his ear. Conway went out, and soon returned with a superb piece of fresh-peeled bark, with which Mr. Jones was duly covered. "Look here, gentlemen," said he triumphantly, "you may now go to grass with your shed. I wouldn't change places with the man in the middle." The shed replied with a shout of laughter and a storm of jokes. "He's fairly embarked in it," cried another. "Looks more like he was embalmed," cried another. "A mummy! or a mud-turtle lying on his back—Pharaoh the Fat! I'd like to see Gliddon unroll him before the Historical Society of Massachusetts." "Rail on from your mud-hole, my good fellows; but take my advice, and reserve your wit, for it will require more than you have got among you to keep yourselves dry to-night. I am entirely impervious either to jokes or rain; good-night." Unfortunately for Mr. Jones's comfort the wind changed, and the rain poured upon him in rivulets; and shortly afterward groans and lamentations were heard in the direction of the mummy. "It seems to be in pain; some one had better look after it," said X. Conway good-naturedly took a chunk of fire and went to Mr. Jones's assistance. It turned out that the acrid sap from the hemlock-bark had got into his eye; but it was soon over, and a deep sleep fell upon them all—which lasted until the wood-robin warbled a reveille on the following morning. When they awoke it was still raining, and from all appearances had been raining hard all night. A thin vapory smoke rose from the extinguished embers, and all nature was dripping.

"By the beard of the Prophet!" exclaimed Porte Crayon as he combed the leaves and sticks out of his own flowing appendage, "by the beard of Mahomet, I have been sleeping all night in a puddle of water."

"The hydrostatic bed," said Mr. Smith, "is preferable to any other for an invalid."

"Well done, Smith, this is the first time we've heard from you since night before last. You must be getting better."

"Thank you, I feel much better, and will hereafter be a believer in the water cure."

"Look here," said X., sticking his heels into the air, while a stream poured from each boot.

"Bless my soul!" quoth Mr. Penn emphatically, as he gathered up his legs and arms like separate pieces of lumber, and scrutinized the covering of the shed; "there must be a leak in this roof; the water has been dribbling into my left ear, until it is so full I can't hear." Just then a drop took him in the eye. "There! blast the thing, I was sure of it."

"Conway! Conway! my good friend, come here," cried a sepulchral voice.

"Hark from the tombs—the mummy desires to be uncased."

"No—stand back. I don't want any of your aid—Conway, good fellow, remove this confounded bark. Gently—there—now help me to bend my legs—oh!—ah!—whew!—thank you—let go now, I think I can stand alone"; and, after sundry efforts, Mr. Jones recovered the use of his legs sufficiently to carry him to breakfast, where, by a free use of fried middling and hot coffee, he lubricated his limbs into their usual condition of activity.

A council of war decided that the army was not in condition to move on that day, and that they should remain under cover, and repose while such as felt disposed should go out as scouts to explore thoroughly the surrounding country. Conway's talents were again called in requisition to extend and improve the comfort of their quarters. A pack of cards was introduced, and the day passed in careless jollity. During the forenoon, Porte Crayon accompanied by Powell went out to search for the Cheat River, but after walking in idle circles for two hours, and becoming entangled in a laurel-brake, they were glad to get back to camp. Dindon, Thornhill, and Powell were more successful, and returned late in the evening with the report that they had found the Cheat, and had wounded an otter. This news gave great satisfaction, but their description of the stream differed so widely from the supposed location and size of that river, that the accuracy of the report was doubted by Mr. Penn and others who had been studying the geography of the country.

The fourth morning proved a favorable one. The sun rose bright and clear, and our adventurers, refreshed in body and soul, resumed their journey with cheerful alacrity. After marching about a mile, an extensive laurel-brake seemed to offer an impassable barrier to their further progress. Here the scouts of the previous evening informed them that the river flowed through the laurel some two or three hundred yards distant, upon which information a convenient spot was selected for a permanent encampment. Conway, Dindon, and Thornhill undertook to build the house, while the rest of the party started eagerly to explore the river and have a day's sport. After traversing the thicket, they reached a stream about forty feet wide, and of inconsiderable depth, completely hemmed in by laurel and beautifully arched with evergreens, so dense and dark that it had a cavernous look.

"This stream is certainly not the Cheat River," said Mr. Penn.

Powell suggested that it might be the Canaan Fork.

"There is no such stream known to geographers," said Mr. Penn.

"It is the same," rejoined Powell, "that we ignorant hunters have been accustomed to call by that name, and it empties into the Cheat not far from here, I should say."

"By the maps this stream has no right to be here at all," continued Mr. Penn. "Either the maps or the stream must be mistaken. My map is a very correct map, I don't like to doubt its authority, but I suppose I must defer to the stream. Here it is. Now for the exploration."

The party, headed by Crayon, straggled down the bed of the stream, sometimes waist deep, sometimes ankle deep, climbing or dodging the enormous tree trunks that bridged it at short intervals. On turning a rocky bend, the stream with its green archway disappeared as if by some trick of magic, and a bright open landscape of mountain sides and distant hazy tops suddenly occupied its place. Beneath their feet yawned an unfathomable chasm, from whose misty depths rose a confused sound of rushing waters. The hemlocks below looked like shrubs. Into this abyss the wild stream leaped, falling into a black pool

scintillating with foam and bubbles. Here it seemed to tarry for a moment to gather strength for another and more desperate plunge; then another and another, down! down! down!—and down went the explorers, shouting, leaping, sliding, and tumbling, catching the spirit of the scene, until they seemed as wild and reckless as the torrent. Tarry upon this shelving platform of rock and look up. A succession of silvery cascades seem falling from the clouds; the pines which we saw beneath our feet now rise clear and diminutive against the blue sky. Below, the stream still pours down the yawning chasm. We can see it foaming far down, until rocks and trees are dim in the distance. Here's a clear leap of fifty feet; what's to be done? Can we go no farther? The trunk of a fallen hemlock has lodged against the rocky ledge. It stands at a perilous angle, and its decayed surface is covered with green and slippery ooze. Who cares! down we slide one after another. What next?—a shorter jump on the opposite side is a tangled thicket of rhododendron; to reach it we must cross a bridge fearful as the arch of Al-Sirat, a slender trunk that has drifted across the furious current. Hurrah! The Ravels could not have done it better. Now swing down the laurels—not all at once, or they will break. Push on, boys! the great foaming caldron below must be the river.

"There seems to be no way but this," said Porte, resolutely jumping upon a drifted trunk that projected full thirty feet over the ledge into the topmost branches of a lofty beech. He gained the tree in safety, and descended to the shore of the river; the others followed in rapid succession, although the dangerous bridge swayed and shook with each passenger. "Jones, don't try it!—Jones, you're too heavy—it shakes, it cracks—by Heaven, he's gone!"

With a sullen crash the heavy log fell into the pool below, while the intrepid Jones slid down the friendly beech, amid the bravos and felicitations of his comrades. Jones sat panting on a rock, red with exertion, beaded with perspiration, all saturated with water, and green with ooze. What a miraculous change? Can that be the same being that hung to old Kit's tail, or that groaned so lustily when he got sap in his eye? Jones, who crossed the bridge with the step of a rope-dancer? and who walked the drift-log with the courage of a Delhi? O Nature! How mighty are thy influences upon the impressible souls of men. How surely do thy softer beauties woo to luxury and indolence the same spirits who, amid thy rocks and thundering cataracts, are roused to energy and active daring. The Black Fork of Cheat, where our party stood, was about two hundred feet in width, and poured its amber flood at an angle of some seven or eight degrees, over a bed of monstrous boulders, and between mountain walls a thousand or twelve hundred feet in height.

"It looks to me," said X., "like the bursting of Barclay and Perkins's big beer-tub, you remember, that flooded half London, and drowned so many people."

"I wish to heaven it was beer," said Jones; "I think I could drink a barrel of it on the spot."

Such was the excitement and exhilaration produced by the discovery of these beautiful falls, that fishing became for the time a secondary object, and but few trout were caught. Penn and Smith, however, could not long resist the desire of trying their fine rods. Having uncased and fitted them up, they made a simultaneous throw. Smith's foot slipped, and he came down upon the point of his rod, splintering it to the last joint. Penn made a magnificent fling, but having forgotten to attach his line to the reel, three of the joints went over the falls, carrying with them the sea grass line and that incredible specimen of entomology, the bug.

Having disposed of his rod to his complete satisfaction, Smith proposed to Crayon that they should make an exploration of the river, following its course downward toward the mouth of the Blackwater. They persevered in this undertaking until they had accomplished some two or three miles, but finding the route scarcely less difficult and hazardous than the descent of the falls, and having in the meantime emptied their haversacks, they concluded to return and rejoin their comrades. They found them waiting at the foot of the falls, tired of fishing, which had been unsuccessful, owing to the swollen condition of the stream.

The ascent of the falls was accomplished with more circumspection and with less danger than the descent. The precipices were avoided by scrambling up on the mountain-sides through the laurel, and the explorers rejoined the Building Committee early in the afternoon. As they approached the spot, each one was big with the scenes and adventures of the day, and thirsting to begin the narrative of his personal experiences and exploits. They suddenly drew up, like men bewildered, and then gave a simultaneous shout of pleasure and admiration.

"Hurrah for Conway!—Hurrah for Dindon!—Hurrah for Thornhill! Well, this out-does the wonders of the Canaan Fork!" exclaimed X.

Before them stood a neat and roomy cottage complete at all points, with an open front, before which blazed a glorious fire. The baggage all securely and neatly bestowed, with shelves and fixtures for the cooking utensils, a rack at the fire for drying clothes, and, indeed, every comfort and convenience that could have been desired, and more than could have been reasonably hoped for. Conway sat philosophically smoking his pipe at the entrance; Thornhill was cooking supper; and Mr. Dindon, with a hospitable wave of the hand, desired them to walk in, make themselves at home, and take a bite of supper with him.

It was creditable to the exploring party that not a word was said in relation to their own adventures until the full meed of praise had been bestowed upon the builders for the ingenuity and industry which they had manifested in the accomplishment of their work. The enjoyment of the evening, however, was dampened by the unfavorable accounts of the condition of the river, and the diminished chances for sport. That night the mercury in Porte Crayon's pocket thermometer stood at 32°;

and notwithstanding the well-nourished fire and comfortable shelter, it was impossible to sleep on account of the cold. That night also finished Mr. Jones. The reaction from the enthusiasm of the previous day, combined with the cold and loss of rest, brought the mercury of his spiritual thermometer below zero. Powell was to start that morning with the horses for the settlements. After partaking of a hearty breakfast, Mr. Jones formally announced his intention of accompanying them. Without regarding the exclamations of surprise which the announcement called forth, he proceeded as follows:

"A decent respect for the opinions of the world makes it necessary that I should give my reasons for this step. There are briefly these: I came out here for sport and pleasure; I have found neither. I have been out five days, and have not caught five trout; I have been tired to death, and unable to sleep—saturated, frozen, devoured by gnats and wood-ticks."

"And got sap in your eye," suggested Mr. Dindon.

"And besides, instead of venison and trout, I have been gorged with fried bacon and biscuit, until I am sick of seeing them."

"Three times five makes fifteen," said X. "He has been gorged just fifteen times, to say nothing of snacks and odd biscuits. Poor fellow! how he must have suffered!"

"And," pursued Mr. Jones, in a louder key, "I pronounce the expedition a failure and a humbug; and, consequently, I will return with Powell."

Several hasty remarks were half-uttered, when Porte Crayon rose and affectionately addressed Mr. Jones:

"In expressing my deep regret at your sudden departure, let me assure you that I am heartily seconded by every one here present—a regret that would have been felt under any circumstances, but which is doubly felt when we remember the gallant and spirited Mr. Jones of yesterday. And let me also express a hope that the acrimonious character of your remarks is the result of physical discomfort, rather than of any unkind feeling toward this party or any member of it."

"Not a trace of it!" warmly responded Mr. Jones; "quite the contrary, I assure you all. I was wrong to say any thing against the enterprise. You all have enjoyed it, I have no doubt; but I will confess I'm not fit for this life; I'm—I am—friendship demands the sacrifice, and I'll out with the truth: I'm too confounded fat!"

A shout of approbation followed the avowal.

"Jones, my dear fellow, your hand! Let's have a cordial embrace all round."

They started off—when Jones suddenly turned about. "Ah, X., my friend, come here! You were kind enough to make a calculation for me when I was speaking; it was civil of you. As I am going home, and you will probably have a great deal of walking to do before you return, I'll make you a present of my extra-boots. Adieu!"

How Mr. Jones walked until he was out of sight, and then mounted Lame Kit; how he had a surprising adventure with a hen-pheasant; and how he got safe back to the settlements, have nothing to do with this narrative, and consequently will be considered as not having been alluded to at all.

The parties who went out to try the streams again soon returned unsuccessful and disappointed, and betook themselves to "all-fours" for the remainder of the day. Conway, however, who had gone over to the Blackwater, returned with about a hundred and fifty fine trout. This lucky forage afforded the company a couple of hearty meals, and determined them to leave their present location, and seek a more favorable one on the Blackwater; not, however, without many expressions of regret at deserting their fine cabin.

On the following morning they marched about four miles, and came upon the Blackwater Creek, about a mile above the falls. As they followed down the bed of the stream, a deer was seen to cross a short distance from them, which so excited Mr. X. that he made a rush to get ahead of the main body, and, if possible, to get a shot. Just as he was about attaining his object, he set foot upon a slippery stone, and pitched head-foremost into the water. As he emerged, his gun spouting from both barrels, he was hailed with shouts of encouragement.—"There goes the deer!—shoot! bang away!" X. politely requested the company to go to a place where cold water was more of a rarity; and quietly took his position in the rear of the column.

The site chosen for the new encampment was on the brow of a cliff, within thirty paces of the great fall—a situation of unequaled beauty and savage grandeur. Surrounded by a tangled thicket of the rhododendron, canopied by the loftiest firs, the thunder of the cataract in their ears day and night, and its spray freshening the atmosphere they breathed, our adventurers passed the eight days that followed in the fullest enjoyment of the pleasures of forest-life. Every day added to the treasures of Porte Crayon's sketch-book. The author reveled in a poetic existence, basking on moss-covered rocks, among foaming rapids and sparkling waterfalls; and if his haggard and unshaven countenance and dilapidated wardrobe presented a strong contrast to his mental beatitude, it only exemplified the more strikingly the predominance of mind over matter, and the entire disconnection that sometimes exists between the ideal and the material world.

On the first favorable day after their location, X. M. C., who had not yet fleshed his maidenhook in the gills of a trout, went out with Conway to try his luck. After many unsuccessful attempts, he at length hooked a fellow and drew him out of the water with such a jerk (X. is possessed of great physical vigor), that rod, line, and fish were lodged in the overhanging branches of a tree. Here was a spite—the stream was wriggling with trout, and X. had just acquired the knack of hooking them; but his implements, and, worse than all, the first trophy of his skill, were hanging on the envious boughs. Now, if X. M. C. had any one trait that predominated over all others, it was determination. Missiles were plenty, and he straightway opened upon the devoted fish a mingled shower of stones, sticks, and anathemas. At the end of an hour he succeeded in bringing him down, well dried and slightly tainted.

"Well!" quoth Conway, who, from a short distance had been the philosophical eye-witness of the proceeding, and who during the time had bagged some sixty of the finest trout—"Well; I've seed fish catched in a great many different ways, but I never seed 'em chunked out of trees afore."

About four o'clock in the afternoon our sportsmen generally gathered in for dinner. There is a kind of seasoning found in these mountain countries which gives to the coarsest food a savor, compared with which Delmonico's *chefs de cuisine* are insipid. Would it not be possible for some of our chemists to make an extract from this sauce, and bottle it for city use? How would your truffles, your mushrooms, your *à la*

Marengo's be blotted from the list of delicacies, and their places filled with *sauce à l'Allegheine* and fried middling, *sauté à l'air de le Montaigne.* After dinner coffee and cards were introduced; and when it became too dark for all fours, "the vaulted aisles of the dim wood rang" with songs, choruses, and recitations; and it is no more than just to state that the neighboring bears had occasionally opportunities of hearing performances that would have challenged the admiration of the most gifted circles in the land.

On rainy days the camp wore quite an air of domesticity. In the centre was the eternal party at "old sledge." The author, wearied with such trite amusement, conned his note-book in the corner; the artist in another, arranged and re-touched his sketches; while old Conway with his jack-knife, passed his time in manufacturing wooden spoons, plates, and water-tight baskets of bark.

Conway was the most accomplished of woodsmen: small in stature, narrow-shouldered, and weasel-faced—insensible to fatigue, to hunger; or the vicissitudes of the weather; a shrewd hunter, a skillful fisher, unfailing in resources, he was ready in every emergency. He could build a comfortable house and furnish it in a day, with no other material than what the forest afforded, and no other tools than his ax and jack-knife. Nor was he destitute of the arts of civilized life. He could mend clothes and cobble shoes with surprising dexterity; and any one who has visited his cabin may have observed an old fiddle hanging beside his powder-horn and pouch. When in camp his pipe was never out; he smoked before and after meals, when at work and when idle. He talked but little, but occasionally told a quaint story of his hunting adventures, or cracked a dry joke; and the sharp twinkle of his gray eye, when anything humorous was in question, showed the keenness of his appreciation of good-natured fun.

Rainy days were also fruitful in debates, which a discreet person might have characterized as noisy wrangles; and as usual the vehemence of the debaters was great in proportion to the littleness of the subject. It must be confessed the range of questions was a wide one—anything from the Constitution of the United States down to the propriety of a play at "old sledge." The parties generally stood arrayed, Mr. Dindon against the field, the field against Mr. Dindon. One day Mr. Dindon was six in the game, and stood on the knave with another trump. Two consecutive leads brought down Mr. Dindon's jack, and he lost the game but characterized his opponent's play as absurd and contrary to Hoyle. The whole pack—not of cards, but of players—opened upon him. The dispute waxed hotter and hotter, and Mr. Dindon waxed redder and redder, and finally lost all command of himself. He glared about him like a baited bear. Suddenly rushing forward, he seized Conway's ax. The debaters scattered and dodged like rats in a pantry; but he deigned not to cast a look upon them, and strode out, upsetting the water-bucket and knocking over the clothes-rack in his progress. Presently he found himself, *vis-à-vis* with an enormous hemlock, full fifteen feet in girth. Without considering the size and vigor of his opponent, he attacked him furiously. He knocked out chips as large as dinner-dishes, and the earth around was soon white with them. For a long time the combat seemed to be equal; the perspiration stood on Dindon's forehead in drops as large as kidney-beans; the inhabitants of the camp stood around at a respectable distance, dodging the chips and wondering. Anon the lofty crown of the hemlock was seen to waver, the blows of the ax resounded with redoubled force, the trunk cracked and crackled, and the gigantic forest king began to sink, at first slowly, then with a rushing sound and with a thundering crash like the broadside of a frigate, he fell, crushing under him like shrubs a dozen trees, each of which might have been the pride of a city park.

Dindon wiped his cheerful and unclouded brow, and with an air of careless triumph slung the ax into a log. "There now!" said he, "some of you smart gentlemen may chop that fellow into fire-sticks and carry them to the camp."

"By the body of Hercules!" exclaimed X., as the green wood rang with shouts of applause and triumph: "shade of Milo! I here make a vow never to dispute with Mr. Dindon again on any subject; the fate of that hemlock has convinced me that he can never be wrong, and that the rest of us are poor feeble mortals, after all."

One afternoon the attention of the party in the shed was directed to the external world by the increasing roar of the cataract. It had been drizzling all day, but for an hour or more the rain fell by buckets-full. Some apprehensions were expressed for the safety of Messrs. Penn and

Conway, who were absent on a fishing-excursion. Accordingly, the party all went down to the banks of the stream to look out for the absentees. The Blackwater seemed run mad; and the fall, swelled to treble its usual volume, made the very hills tremble. Quantities of drift were passing, and some shade of real anxiety clouded the faces of the watchers.

"Oh horror!" exclaimed X., "oh, fatal day! there goes Penn's body; there! there! he's over the falls—he's gone!"

"Why," said Thornhill, "that looked to me like a forked stick."

"No," insisted X., "it was Penn. I recognized his legs. I can't be mistaken."

Many kindly regrets were expressed, and eulogies pronounced upon his virtues, talents, and amiable traits—some of which the defunct had the pleasure of overhearing, as he crept out of a laurel thicket, and followed them up the path to the shelter, all forlorn and dripping.

"Why, here comes the gentleman now," said Thornhill.

"Angels and ministers of grace, defend us!" exclaimed X., throwing himself into a superb attitude—

> "Be thou a spirit of health or goblin damn'd,
> Thou com'st in such a questionable shape
> That I will speak to thee.......
> A ghost of shreds and patches. I'll call thee Penn.
> Oh answer me, let me not burst in ignorance; but tell
> How many fish you've caught—and where's the otter?"

"The otter is coming on with the fish," replied the ghost, in a sepulchral voice. "We've got about two hundred. In the meantime, hasten supper. I've had a narrow escape from drowning, and am now perishing with hunger."

At that moment Conway appeared with his load of fish, which were hailed with acclamations.

"Disciple of Izaak Walton!" said X., embracing the dripping body of Mr. Penn, and squeezing him like a sponge in his grateful ecstasy: "may you live forever. Glorious otter! what a fry we'll have!" And Mr. X. forthwith repaired to the fallen hemlock, and furnished himself with the largest chip he could find, to serve as a plate for the anticipated supper.

While this was cooking Mr. Penn seated himself on the end of a log

at the fire, and narrated his adventure. He and Conway had been some distance up the Blackwater, and had been very successful. Mr. Penn was seated on a rock in the middle of the stream, and so intent was he on the sport, that he did not notice either the rain or the rise of the water. (As has been before observed, Mr. Penn has a remarkable gift of abstracting himself from wordly surroundings.) When the water began to pour over the rock on which he was sitting he jumped up, and, to his amazement, found himself hemmed in by the foaming torrent. He made a plunge to gain the nearest bank, lost his footing, and was washed up like a piece of drift among some rocks. Here he found himself on the wrong side. The appearance of the stream was terrific, but the terror of an unsheltered and supperless night was greater. Presently he saw Conway on the other side, making unintelligible signs to him. He rushed into the water up to his arm-pits; but it looked like suicide to go on, and he struggled back to the bank. Then a large tree drifted by and lodged against the rocks, forming a temporary bridge that reached nearly across. The thought of supper braced him to the desperate venture, and he leaped upon the log. With his weight the end upon which he jumped broke loose, and swung rapidly round like a flying ferry, bringing him within reach of the laurels on the opposite side. Mr. Penn grasped the bushes, and saved himself—while the tree, loosed from its moorings hurried on toward the falls.

"This I consider a very respectable adventure," said Mr. Penn, handing over his tin cup for his second pint of coffee, and deliberately separating the rich salmon flakes from the spinal column of a large trout. Deliberately, we say, for Mr. Penn was then on his fourteenth fish.

But all things must come to an end sooner or later. The party were all gathered under the bark roof—some smoking, others conversing in a more quiet and serious tone than had been usual among them. X. M. C. finally spoke out.

"Friends, and fellow-woodmen," said he, "our sojourn in the wilderness is about to end. We have promised to be at Towers' on the 16th. To fulfill this promise we must start homeward to-morrow morning. Owing to the early departure of Mr. Jones, we still have an abundance of provision, and might, if we were so disposed, remain a week longer, but the council seem to have determined on going. Well, let it be so. We have not realized all our expectations on coming out. We have killed neither bear, panther, nor deer. We have not even varied our diet with cat-fish soup—(nodding to Mr. Penn)—but we have manfully carried out the proposed objects of our expedition as far as circumstances permitted. We have explored the wilderness, fished in the Black Fork of Cheat, seen the Falls of the Canaan, surfeited on trout, and braved the unpropitious elements unflinchingly. As for me, the impressions made by this sojourn will never be effaced—never, though I were to live as long as the great hemlock felled by Mr. Dindon."

The return to the settlements was unmarked by any incident worthy of record. Accustomed to the forest, hardened to the toil, the difficulties of the march passed as matters of course; and an occasioned unsuccessful shot at a deer or the discovery of a bear's trail only elicited a brief comment or a laugh. On the second morning they breakfasted at Conway's, dined at Towers', and, twenty-four hours after, the heroes of the Expedition into Canaan had resumed the dress, and, to all appearance, the habits of ordinary life. Yet by a shrewd observer of character they might still be distinguished from the common herd. There was a certain gallant swagger when they walked abroad, a lighting-up of the face when they met each other, or when the subject of hunting and fishing was introduced; an elevation of ideas, a largeness of speech, an ill concealed disdain of the petty affairs of life, such as law, medicine, or agriculture; and for a long time, whenever they were invited out, even the heavy handed and profuse housekeepers of their neighborhood seemed to have suddenly become close and thrifty, or to have made some unaccountable mistake in their calculations.

In the town of M. were several returned Californians who had made the overland trip, dug gold and starved on the Yuba and Feather rivers, and returned to their homes by the Horn or the Isthmus, with nothing to show for their trouble but a stock of hard-earned experience, and the hope of being heroes and story-tellers for the rest of their days. Alas! they happened in an unlucky time. Whenever one of them, thinking he had an audience in a barroom or at a street corner, would commence, *infandum renovare dolorem,* he was invariably trumped with—"Yes, that reminds me of the Blackwater"; and in five minutes the poor Californian stood mute and abashed at supposing that he had ever been hungry in his life, or had ever seen any thing worth talking about.*

---

* Harper's New Monthly Magazine, VIII, 18–36 (Dec., 1853).

Wild Cattle Hunting on Green Island

CHARLES HALLOCK

The kind of terrain which the South has in greater abundance than any other major section of the United States is coastal swampland. As a result, the straying of domestic animals from pastures and fields in the coastal states presented difficulties of more than the usual order. Strayed hogs and cattle in the marsh areas very easily "went wild," and in favorable environments found provender the year round to make them increase in stature and progeny, if not in wisdom. The community hunts organized from time to time to round up or kill them provided a favorite sport. The term *cowboy* possibly originated in the slang designation of the participants in such roundups, long before anyone ever heard of the picturesque horsemen who haunted the Chisholm Trail or roistered in Dodge City saloons. Ropes and pistols were the chief instruments in such ventures, for the operations were necessarily conducted at close quarters, and slaves were assembled to beat the bushes to assist the mounted sportsmen. The dangers involved were exciting enough to attract the boldest spirits; and the eating, too, was an inducement, for a roast loin of pork or a succulent beef steak was to most palates preferable to even the choicest venison. A collection of hunting narratives from the Old South would be incomplete without a sampling of this dangerous sport. Accordingly, there follow two firsthand descriptions of wild cattle hunting, both with a locale in the swamp section of Georgia.

The author of the first piece was Charles Hallock, of old and distinguished New England lineage, who was born in 1834 in New York City, where for many years his father edited the well-known *Journal of Commerce*. After attending Amherst College, he, too, became a newspaper reporter and editor. An ardent outdoorsman, fond of camping, fishing, and hunting, Hallock naturally included the South in his varied sporting junkets, and his first book dealt with the Georgia scene—*The Recluse of the Oconee* (1854). Long before his death in 1917 he was widely recognized as an authority on field sports, fishing, and conservation, and as the author of several hunting and fishing guides. In 1873 he founded one of the leading outdoors magazines, *Forest and Stream,* which he edited for seven years, and later established two other similar periodicals, *Nature's Realm* and *Western Field and Stream.* In 1871 he helped to establish the Bloomington Grove Park Association in Pike County, Pennsylvania, which was often considered the first game preserve in the nation; and three years later he pioneered the International Association for the Preservation of Game. A kind of code which he fathered served as a model for conservation legislation in a number of states. It is obvious that the blood of the old New England reformers still flowed in his veins. Hallock's sketch first appeared in *Harper's Magazine,* to which he was a frequent contributor.

ALL along the coast of Georgia the ocean sets into the land by numerous estuaries, creeks, and inlets, which, intersecting, form an extensive chain of fertile islands of great diversity in size and shape—some, whose large areas are monopolized by flourishing plantations; others densely wooded, with outlines sweeping gracefully into all conceivable curves, girt by the waters that float dreamily by. These are Edenal retreats, tenanted by lithe-limbed deer with large, loving eyes, and gaudy birds that flutter noisily amidst the interwoven foliage. Here the orange and palmetto grow in full luxuriance, the fragrant magnolia and huge live-oaks draped to their summits with long pendent moss; and along the shadowy shores overhanging bushes, festooned with trailing plants, droop to the water's surface. Other islands are but isolated hummocks away out in the ocean, where the surf never ceases to thunder, covered at all times with uncouth wild-fowl waddling over the rocks, noodles, and screaming gulls, while the air above is filled with myriads constantly hovering.

This is the famous Sea Island cotton district, where planters grow wealthy by the cultivation of a staple whose market price is 33 cents per pound; and here are aristocratic estates whose proprietors are "native and to the manor born" of the real old Georgian stock, living in simple but most substantial style, the owners of many negroes and of imported cattle of the purest blood. Here the climate is delightful, and always tempered by the cool breezes wafted from the ocean. The atmosphere has a purplish hazy hue that gives to the eye an uncertain horizon, and the sun shines through with a softened light, such as reposes in the quiet vale of Cashmere, or in

> ". . . that sweet Indian land,
> Whose air is balm:"

a dreamy clime such as would indite impassioned lyrics for harps long since hung on willows.

Of these numerous islands that known as Green Island is the property of an eminent citizen of Georgia. Its whole large area was once a thriving plantation; but of late years it has been suffered to run to waste by its owner, who abandoned it either because he had accumulated sufficient wealth, or that he might devote his time and energies to other pursuits more lucrative or more congenial to his taste, or more for the public good. The single negro family left behind as curators of the estate have not prevented the encroachments of that rank vegetation which always springs from the fallow field, or of the decay that follows neglect. The idle children saunter lazily among the rickety out-buildings and falling fences, or fish in the sluggish creek for mullet, while the old blacks sun themselves in the door-ways in lieu of more arduous duties. There is a luxurious growth of young palmettoes where the fields were once white with cotton blooms, and squads of Berkshire shotes, wild as the boars of Bohemia, roam *ad libitum* and charge desperately into the cassena copses with a quick, sharp grunt when suddenly disturbed. Then there are herds of Devon cattle of aristocratic blood, splendid animals, as wild as the lordly buffaloes of the Western prairies, but far more fierce and dangerous—the multiplied progeny of half a score of their noble kin imported twelve years since, and *then* cognizant of their master's crib, but which were granted the freedom of the island when the estate was abandoned, and now own no liege in man. These have grown wilder and wilder with each successive generation, until their natural fire has flamed into a restless passion, swelling the full veins that traverse their delicate skins, lighting their dark eyes with a malicious brightness, and imparting a nervous quickness to their well-turned limbs. The haughty brutes are at all times ready to charge at whatever may excite their anger, or to dispute territorial possession with every living thing that crosses their path, and in open list would defy the expertest matadores of Spain.

Some time since the herd numbered about one hundred and fifty; but such dainty and precious flesh could not long be permitted to run to grass when the few whitleather sirloins exposed in the shambles were but slanders upon the name of beef. Hence repeated incursions into their domain, and sanguinary assaults by organized bands of hunters, have biennially furnished many rare and juicy tid-bits to titillate epicurean palates and thereby reduced the number of the cattle to some thirty head.

There is no gentleman's "preserve" in all Georgia so redundant in sport so exciting and deliciously dangerous, as is this hunting-ground of Green Island; and they are deemed fortunate who chance to be the recipients of an invitation from its proprietor, or members of his family, to participate in it. What thrill of pleasurable anticipation tingles every vein when the shrill horn calls "to horse!" How the mettled steeds themselves seem to catch the subtle inspiration, champing their impatience, and springing with nervous bound and fluttering pulse; and the whole crew of gathering dogs, of all degrees—bull-dog, hound, and mastiff—darting hither and thither in wild excitement, uttering eager whines and yelps! Then the scurry and scrubrace that brings the huntsmen within sight of the old, dilapidated "quarter," serves to warm the blood the more, and begets a glorious intoxication of animal spirit that nerves them for the dangers of the thickest fray. Once more a blast from the horn winds long and full in the direction of the silent and apparently deserted hamlet; but before its echo has time to answer, a black woolly head peers suddenly up from a stubble patch that had seemed tenantless, gives two or three spasmodic jerks from right to left, then displays for an instant a chasm lined with ivory, and quickly disappears under the heels of its owner, who turns a nimble summersault, and darts away toward the "quarter" with a succession of tremendous bounds and strange contortions of body and limbs.

"Oh keigh! whoop! golly! dar dey come! Come out dat, you niggers! Yeah, Mass' Sam—ole bull tail—de whole of 'em—run cow—golly sakes foreber—dere dey is!"

"Oh, go 'way, you irridiscible soot-bag! What ye want come luff foolin' round heah for, makin' sich a noise? Afeard de cattle, does ye? 'Tink you must be prediwessicated. Keah!"

"Who you call pedessicated, ole Sambo nigger? You jest come 'long, de whole pack ob you chicken-gizzards! If dar ain't all de—"

Again comes a piercing shriek from the horn, near at hand, and followed by a simultaneous yell from all the dogs. This double summons is instantly answered by a bevy of negroes, old and young, who tumble helter-skelter through the door-way and from behind adjacent buildings, while a rabble of leaping curs join chorus with the voices of the newcomers, and run to meet them.

"Oh, *dar* Massa Sam, for sartain; Kurnel George, and young Mass' Dave too, and heap ob gemmen! Mornin'!, gemmen! Yah! yah! de bulls is about dis mornin', and dar's heap ob tracks all 'bout de sinkhole, and plenty ob calfmeat too, Mass' Sam, sence you was down to de island lass fall."

"Yes, massa; and de big bull is more savagous dan he eber was. Golly! what mighty fine hoss! Oats neber kill dat hoss, I spec."

"Shut yer mouf, imperence, Josh, and keep dem ivories close. 'Tink corn-bread break dem teef?"

"Oh, go 'way, 'possum, and don't be so conflution just 'cause you's in gemmen's sciety! Mass' Sam, I tell you dem dogs is anxious for de stwife; an' heah's my pup Sanch—*he* de dog! De big bull gub him toss last fall, but he hold on wid he teef like a curl-tail 'possum to a 'simmon-tree."

"Ki! yah! jist heah dat low-priced nigger talk! Dat ain't no pup! Here, Pomp! dat *my* pup!"

"Dis my Snap—catch um bull."

"An' dis Hannibal—*he* a pup!"

"An' dis—"

"There, now! George, did you ever hear such a chattering flock of lunatic crows in all your life? Silence, the whole of you, lazy hounds! You ought to be at work in a sugar-mill instead of idling here. Brother

William always was very easy with his servants, and these good-for-nothing boys here have had it all their own way until they have become as wild as the very cattle themselves. Away with you! don't stand there bowing and grinning. Ah! I understand now what you want. One might suppose you hadn't seen a dime in ten years. There! Now clear out, the whole of you, if you don't want to feel the snapper of this whip; and put out the dogs, and see if you can't start out those cattle. Here, Sambo!"

"Yes, massa!"

"You take Tom and the best of the dogs and go down to the bayou, and if the cattle are there, drive them up to the more open ground where we can get a fair crack at them. Do you hear?"

"Yes, massa. Trust ole Sambo to dat. Science shall prewail ober all obstaclums."

"And you, Picaninny Joe, run and tell old Marm Sallie to have a lunch ready for us when we come back; and tell her to prepare it in her best style, for we shall be hungry as wolves."

"Yes, Sah, I'se goin' straight."

Old Sambo was the patriarch of a numerous family, as the dog Sanch was of all the mongrels on the premises. Sam was the prototype of Sanch. More than sixty years had laid him siege, and with the wrinkles that seamed his skinny face, and the gray that mottled his fleece of wool, had also added a dignity and self-complacency which were manifested by a benignant rolling of the whites of his eyes, and occasional broad grins, more of condescension than of mirth. And if there were aught of meaning in the formal wag of Sanch's tail, or the indifferent manner in which he received the obstreperous fawnings of the young dogs, or startled them into propriety by a stately snarl, it was easy of interpretation. Hence the twain are officially recognized as law and gospel on all occasions, especially in matters appertaining to the hunting of beasts, the catching of fish, or the entrapping of birds.

Thus Sambo, being duly commissioned, undertook the performance of the duties allotted to him, while the horsemen clattered away to take their stand in waiting for the expected herd. No leather-clad hunter of the Far West was ever more properly equipped and armed than they; for each carried a pair of six-shooting revolvers and a heavy knife, and

one or two had long barreled rifles; but these were intended more for certain contingencies than for active and general use. The pistols were the weapons to do the work, for the encounter was to be hand to hand, and the steaks to be won were large. The horses were apparently trained hunters, mettlesome, and fully imbued with the spirit of the occasion, while their riders would have done credit to a centaur lineage. That "Massa Sam" was as reckless and daring a fellow as ever bestrode a saddle, as agile as a cat, a fine marksman, and as expert a horseman as any Comanche. Many a hairbreadth escape had he already had from the infuriated bulls on this same island, and all the negroes paid due reverence to his prowess. His companions were kindred spirits, and all impatient for the sport of the coming fray.

The sluggish moments are endured with becoming patience, until at last the hunters begin to grow restless under the suspense, when all at once the sharp toot-toot of old Sambo's cow-horn rings out lustily, and the distant deep-mouthed bay of Sanch's well-known voice announces that the noble game is afoot. Then in one short instant more the exhilarating sounds are succeeded by an opening chorus from the whole pack. A momentary pause, broken only by the monotonous baying of a single dog, and another simultaneous roar of fitful yells comes nearer and clearer than before, and with increasing cadence. The sound is electrifying: the horses shiver with eagerness, and with ready alacrity bound away to advantageous points, the better to intercept the chase. Yet another long full blast from the cow-horn, and another chorus of yells and cries from the dogs.

"Hurrah, boys, hurrah! There they come! Now look well to bit and spur! Hurrah for cross-ribs and tender-loins!"

Now the chase bursts into full view through an opening in the trees—the bellowing cattle, some twenty in all, leading the van, and plunging desperately forward in headlong terror; the dogs following closely with deafening clamor, and after them all the darkeys, big and little, afoot and mounted, rushing forward with ear-splitting yells and in tumbling confusion.

"Steady now, steady! Look out for yourselves. Give no quarter."

"That's the word. Give none; but take all the quarters we can."

"Hurrah! now's our time."

The first onslaught has now commenced in real earnest, and the hunters, reckless of danger, dash in together amidst the surging tumult of horns and heels. The cattle, hitherto flying affrighted from an undefined danger, now charge savagely at their foes, since they have assumed a tangible shape ("present fears are less than horrible imaginings"); but the well-trained steeds skillfully elude the desperate brutes by a quick side motion, and, wheeling, follow on in swift pursuit. Crack after crack of pistol-shots is heard in quick succession, and the herd, now scattered, drive crashing through the young palmettoes in all directions, each followed by a rabble of curs, biting and snapping at his heels and flanks, now pausing for an instant in his flight to charge upon his tormentors with stiffened neck, full front, and glaring eyes, tossing them like shuttlecocks from right to left, and then dashing away in the vain attempt to escape them. All is now one general melée—hunters, negroes, cattle, dogs, all mingled in wild confusion—each for himself, and *"sauve qui peut,"* if worst comes to the worst. One huge bull has already measured his length upon the earth, and the gallant Sam comes flying back just opportunely to rescue the "irridiscible" Josh from the fan-like top of a short palmetto, into which he had scrambled for refuge from an infuriated animal, and where he now clung for dear life, the big brute meanwhile butting the quivering tree with such sturdy and determined blows as would soon have shaken the trembling darkey from his perch, in spite of the persistent attacks of sundry small dogs upon his exposed flanks. A couple of well-directed shots brought the bull to his knees, when Josh immediately took his revenge by cutting his hamstrings with his knife.

And now a horse comes careering wildly over the ground, riderless, with great clots of blood flecking his side. The battle has raged fiercely in some quarter. Ha! it's the Colonel's horse, and yonder is the Colonel himself, measuring the ground with colossal strides, and a horn of a most unpleasant dilemma in dangerous proximity to his coat-skirts. There is apparently little chance of escape with a whole skin, for there is no friendly hand near to aid him, and this bovine demonstration is evidently no feint. With head bowed low, tail in air, eyes flashing with rage, and bellowing with revengeful ire, he pushes his victim to the death. The dogs, however, are doing their best; for old Sanch has him by the muzzle, and there is a sturdy bull-terrier hanging from each ear, like huge ear-drops from the auricles of a South Sea Islander; others with their fangs fixed in his pasterns; and another still with firm clutch upon the tuft of his tail, spinning like a teetotum and yelping frantically as he is jerked forward with each convulsive bound of the desperate animal. That bull, with his parasites, would make a spirited sketch for a ready artist, should he desire to give him "a brush."

Darkey Josh regarded the horse with orbs fixed in amazement as he bounded past; but the instant his eye caught sight of the distant struggle his inky face changed suddenly to the color of chocolate and milk, and he threw up his arms with frantic gesture.

"Oh, Mass' Sam, Mass' Sam! dat *de big bull!* Golly sakes for eber! de bery debbil in dat bull. De bullet neber hurt um, and he neber care shucks for all de dogs in Georgy. Bress de Lor', he be witched wid de spook as I'se a libin' nigger! Oh, Massa George, Massa George, dat de big bull should hab you so!"

But "Mass' Sam" didn't pause to listen to this peroration, but, putting spurs to his horse, dashed away in the hope of rescuing his friend from his imminent danger, and Josh instinctively followed after, as quickly as his shuffling feet could carry him. The bull had so lessened the little distance between himself and the object of his pursuit that the unfortunate hunter now felt his hot breath full upon his bare neck behind; indeed, the brute was in the very act of lowering his huge head to give the requisite pitch to the quaver that was to toss his victim high in the air, when the Colonel, with remarkable presence of mind, took advantage of the proximity of a stout palmetto, and threw himself headlong behind the friendly refuge, while the foiled bull, with a howl of baffled rage, swept furiously by. To Sam and Josh this act seemed far from voluntary, and as the prostrate man still lay panting and breathless upon the ground they dared not hope that he had escaped scathless. As they reached the spot the negro's face changed to a hue more pallid than before, and throwing himself upon the body of his master, he gave way to a paroxysm of grief.

"Oh, bress de Lor', bress de Lor'! Massa George is done gone dead for sartin; Oh, Lor', take dis mizzible nigger to heself! Oh, Massa George! de Lor's will be done! dis misery in my bosom almos' brokes my heart. I can hardly perspire. I see de heabens open. Oh, Lor', dis anguished nigger is ready to go!"

These ludicrous appeals and unfeigned tokens of affection were too much for the naturally jovial Colonel, who had a full appreciation for good jokes; and now, partially recovered from his exhaustion, with one desperate effort he threw the wailing negro from him, and springing to his feet, cried, with a well-affected tone of austerity, "Off from me, with your big lubberly carcass! Do you want to crush me to death? I'll teach you manners, boy. I'll make you perspire to your heart's content. Away with you!"

Then, observing the negro's blended look of horror and astonishment, he fell helplessly upon the grass, and gave way to an uncontrollable and prolonged fit of laughter. At these evidences of reanimation Josh's ashy face began to assume its natural hue, and the color gradually came back in streaks, like the wave-marks upon the sandy sea-shore. Still he gazed for a moment half-incredulously; and soon penetrating the other's duplicity, and half-vexed at his own ill-timed display of feeling, said, quietly, in a serio-comic style, "Pshaw! I *knowed* you was only foolin', Massa George! Dem 'possum tricks don't go down wid dis chile. Yah! yah! Dat big bull de very debbil!"

Then, as if uncertain that he had not exceeded the bounds of propriety, he gave one or two spasmodic leaps, and darted from the place. But a kindly summons called him back, and directly, with a silver coin glittering in his palm, he started off for the delinquent horse. The Colonel was not hurt in the least, though he confessed himself badly scared. His steed fared worse, though he was found not dangerously hurt; and the big bull was discovered among those that had "bit the dust," when the noble quarry was counted at the close of the hunt, with more balls in him than ever he had "spooks." He had succumbed at last, to the infinite delight of all the negroes, who had ever regarded him with mingled terror and superstition.

And now, with renewed energy, the whole party, content with blood, essayed to capture alive other members of the numerous family. There was a large pen, or cow-yard, near the farm-house, which had formerly been used for herding the cattle, and which was still amply strong for present use. Into this it was proposed to drive some half a dozen of the full-grown animals for future disposal. As for the yearling calves, of which there were several, these were to be taken with the lasso; and the sport thus afforded would be sufficiently exciting, and far less dangerous than that which they had just enjoyed. It was the *chile con carne*—the dessert after the more substantial meal. Oh, that was the *ne plus ultra* of wild hunts—the chasing of those lithe-limbed calves, as agile as the springbok, through the palmetto copses; in the oft-foiled endeavor to throw the lasso over their knotty, stubborn heads; and in parrying or eluding the brunt of their incipient ferocity, which they had imbibed into their nature with the maternal milk! And after the long and exciting race, in which the third of these bovine bantlings had baffled every attempt at capture—when, at length, the redoubtable Sam, vexed and chagrined, seized the contumacious brute by the extremity of its caudal appendage, and threw himself bodily from his horse over the back of the running calf, thus bearing it to the ground by his own heavy weight, and thereby enabling his comrade to pass the rope over its neck—*that* was the crowning glory of that day's success!

. . . "Come *weal*, come woe,
To peril or overcome the foe!"

The record of that hunt should be bound in calf, and perpetuated for succeeding generations.

Neither was the "surround" and the driving of the unruly cattle into the pen a pastime of any ordinary character; for in this all participated to their heart's content. The cordon of hunters, negroes, dogs, and horses was gradually contracted until within the small space encircled the entangled herd ran, bellowing, swaying, and crushing upon each other, amidst the dust-clouds of their own collision; then made one desperate charge to break the lines of their captors, and in spite of every effort to prevent—in spite of the unearthly din of whoops, cries, yells, the barking of dogs, and firing of guns—succeeded in making good their escape, all but five unfortunates. These were urged within the precincts of the pen, and Sam, the hero of many battles, hastened to lift the bars to their places. One, the topmost, was raised to its socket; and he was in the act of stooping to lift another, when one of the impounded bulls, chancing to catch a glimpse of this unwonted attitude, charged upon him with downward head, passed under the bar and over his prostrate body, and would have escaped scot-free had not Sam—with intuitive quickness, grasped him by the tail. The hinderance was slight, and the delay of short duration; but from some defect in the animal's anatomy, or owing to a vulgar pedigree from the stump-tail breed, the hirsute ornament slipped from its natural fastenings and remained in the victor's hand! And thereby "hangs a tail." This was a becoming finis to the wild cattle hunt on Green Island.

As regards the feast prepared by old Marm Sallie's skill—the corn bread, broiled chickens, fruit, and small beer—the digestive organs duly performed their functions in all matters thereto pertaining.*

* *Harper's New Monthly Magazine*, XXI, 220–224 (July, 1860).

Spearing a Wild Bull

B. H.

"B. H.," the second author who wrote of wild cattle, cannot be identified. He was probably a Georgia planter. His account of spearing a wild bull with a lance appeared in the *American Turf Register,* a popular journal which featured news of horses and horse racing. Letters recounting unusual events associated with hunting or fishing appeared in considerable number in racing and agricultural periodicals and offered the amateur a ready avenue to print. Before the War Between the States quite a few such epistles came from residents in the area below the Potomac. Hunting with the lance as described by "B. H." was more common in the old days than one might suppose, for there are other records of similar hunts. Indeed, the European wild boar was imported into Tennessee by a planter who wished to continue in the New World the lance hunting which he had learned as a youth in Poland. The progeny of his original imports is still sufficiently numerous to warrant an open season on wild boar in both Tennessee and North Carolina.

Southern sportsmen, however, used the lance more frequently as an exercise in horsemanship than as a means of killing game. At local fairs and horse races in many communities a very popular feature was the so-called tournament, in which riders vied with one another in using tapered lances to pick off rings suspended from a succession of poles. Frequently, in medieval or Sir Walter Scott style, the contestants assumed romantic names like the Knight of Franklin County or the Knight of Bellevue Plantation, and gallantly offered their prizes to the Lady of Lost River or the Lady of South Fork Valley, whose colors they wore in the jousting. Such tournaments, alas, have latterly almost entirely disappeared, and the rodeo has begun to take their place.

Jefferson, Camden Co. Geo. Jan. 25, 1832.

In some parts of this country there are many *wild cattle* owned by certain individuals, and so thick and extensive are the swamps in which they range, that they are not under the control of their owners. Sometimes they come out of the swamps to graze in the pine barrens, and in old fields adjoining. Chasing them on horseback, and with dogs, is attended with much risk. They will not turn from their course, unless to attack their pursuers, and will charge without much provocation. The bulls of these wild gangs are large, active, and ferocious, and they are particularly selected by enterprising sportsmen, as the best objects for sport.

A few weeks ago, a small party rode out to hunt these wild bulls, among them was Gen. C. R. Floyd, who carried, on this occasion, a *Polish lance,* to the use of which weapon he had been trained in Europe. The plan was, that he should attack first, and if not successful, the *infallibles* (fire arms) should be used.

The day was calm and clear, and the hunters rode out in fine spirits, accompanied by a large congregation of dogs eager for the fun. After riding several miles, a gang of cattle was discovered in an old field, on the border of a swamp; and among them a fine wild bull of uncommon size, and in the full vigor of life. They soon discovered the party, and dashed for the swamp, raising a fog of dust behind. This was the signal for the attack. Instantly every rein was slack, and the dogs broke forth at the same time in a most delightful cry. The bull, leading the gang, was soon overtaken, although the ground was rough. Gen. F. came up at speed on one of his fine horses, and such was the nature of the ground, and the course of the bull, that he was compelled to approach on the animal's right side, (*the lancer's left*). When within a few feet, with his lance projected, the bull suddenly wheeled from his course and charged the pursuer. He was received on the point of the lance, which entered the whole length of the lance blade, giving him a mortal wound; but the staff, a tough piece of ash, was broken in pieces, a piece about five feet long remaining in the lancer's hand. This did not check the furious enemy, onward he pressed with his wrinkled forehead lowered, ready to plunge his horns in the lancer's horse, and they seemed almost in contact with that noble animal, when by a sudden and active bound in an oblique direction, he placed himself and his rider beyond the thrust of the bull's horns, which missed him but a few inches.

The enraged bull now in turn became the pursuer, and continued his chase for a considerable distance, the lance blade fixed in him, and the *banderolle* waving at his side, from a fragment of the staff.

One of the sportsmen aimed a gun to check his progress, but it *snapped,* and he had to *"stick spurs"* for his own safety. The bull, finding that he could not overtake his enemies, plunged into the swamp, and was followed by Leader, Rainbow, Trooper, Trail, Dido, Gypsey, Sootbag, and other dogs of renown, close at his heels. These four-footed allies soon brought him to bay, the huntsmen went in with their guns, and the hero was soon slain.

N. B. Gen. C. R. F. has, to my knowledge, killed many animals with the lance, and among them a wild boar on the charge; the lance passed through the boar's skull, and killed him on the spot.*

---
* *American Turf Register,* V, 397–399 (April, 1834).

Pitting of Wolves

JOHN JAMES AUDUBON

Next to fire-hunting and trespassing, the topic which elicited the largest number of laws bearing on hunting in early days was varmints. In 1669, for example, the Virginia Burgesses enacted a law requiring the Indians in the colony to kill wolves as tribute. It was decreed that the 725 hunters or bowmen of the various "tributary" villages should be assessed 145 wolves per year. When this effort failed in its purpose the Indians were given bounties instead. But payments for carcasses, scalps, or ears brought on a veritable shower of troubles, for the wily redskins found it easier to hunt the animals in areas far removed from the White settlements, thus defeating the purpose of the law, and even spared the bitches so as to keep a ready supply coming on for the future. In 1790 the Virginia legislature required every free male who was tithable to turn in a certain number of the scalps of crows and squirrels. Everywhere the killing of varmints was in order, with or without bounties, and any and every means was employed to rid plantations or settlements of depredators. Trapping wolves and panthers in pits was a favorite method, probably originally learned from the Indians, who had used it, even to catch buffaloes, from time immemorial.

The author of this account was John James Audubon (1785–1851) whose eminence as a painter of birds has made his name almost synonymous with the word *ornithologist*. He was also an enthusiastic hunter, a man intimately acquainted with the ways of small farmers and large plantation owners, from Kentucky to Florida. The episode is taken from his *Ornithological Biography* (1835), a text prepared as commentary to accompany the hand-colored plates of his *Birds of America* (1827–38).

Pitting of Wolves

THERE seems to be a universal feeling of hostility among men against the Wolf, whose strength, agility, and cunning, which latter is scarcely inferior to that of his relative master Reynard, tend to render him an object of hatred, especially to the husbandman, on whose flocks he is ever apt to commit depredations. In America, where this animal was formerly abundant, and in many parts of which it still occurs in considerable numbers, it is not more mercifully dealt with than in other parts of the world. Traps and snares of all sorts are set for catching it, while dogs and horses are trained for hunting the Fox. The Wolf, however, unless in some way injured, being more powerful and perhaps better winded than the Fox, is rarely pursued with hounds or any other dogs in the open chase; but as his depredations are at times extensive and highly injurious to the farmer, the greatest exertions have been used to exterminate his race. Few instances have occurred among us of any attack made by Wolves on man, and only one has come under my own notice.

Two young Negroes who resided near the banks of the Ohio, in the lower part of the State of Kentucky, about twenty-three years ago, had sweethearts living on a plantation ten miles distant. After the labours of the day were over, they frequently visited the fair ladies of their choice, the nearest way to whose dwelling lay directly across a great cane brake. As to the lover every moment is precious, they usually took this route, to save time. Winter had commenced, cold, dark, and forbidding, and after sunset scarcely a glimpse of light or glow of warmth, one might imagine, could be found in that dreary swamp, excepting in the eyes and bosoms of the ardent youths, or the hungry Wolves that prowled about. The snow covered the earth, and rendered them more easy to be scented from a distance by the famished beasts. Prudent in a certain degree, the young lovers carried their axes on their shoulders, and walked as briskly as the narrow path would allow. Some transient glimpses of light now and then met their eyes, but so faint were they that they believed them to be caused by their faces coming in contact with the slender reeds covered with snow. Suddenly, however, a long and frightful howl burst upon them, and they instantly knew that it proceeded from a troop of

hungry, perhaps desperate Wolves. They stopped, and putting themselves in an attitude of defence, awaited the result. All around was dark, save a few feet of snow, and the silence of night was dismal. Nothing could be done to better their situation, and after standing a few minutes in expectation of an attack, they judged it best to resume their march; but no sooner had they replaced their axes on their shoulders, and begun to move, than the foremost found himself assailed by several foes. His legs were held fast as if pressed by a powerful screw, and the torture inflicted by the fangs of the ravenous animal was for a moment excruciating. Several Wolves in the mean time sprung upon the breast of the other Negro, and dragged him to the ground. Both struggled manfully against their foes; but in a short time one of them ceased to move, and the other, reduced in strength, and perhaps despairing of maintaining his ground, still more of aiding his unfortunate companion, sprung to the branch of a tree, and speedily gained a place of safety near the top. The next morning, the mangled remains of his comrade lay scattered around on the snow, which was stained with blood. Three dead Wolves lay around, but the rest of the pack had disappeared, and Scipio, sliding to the ground, took up the axes, and made the best of his way home, to relate the sad adventure.

About two years after this occurrence, as I was travelling between Henderson and Vincennes, I chanced to stop for the night at a farmer's house by the side of a road. After putting up my horse and refreshing myself, I entered into conversation with mine host, who asked if I should like to pay a visit to the wolf-pits, which were about half a mile distant. Glad of the opportunity, I accompanied him across the fields to the neighbourhood of a deep wood, and soon saw the engines of destruction. He had three pits, within a few hundred yards of each other. They were about eight feet deep, and broader at bottom, so as to render it impossible for the most active animal to escape from them. The aperture was covered with a revolving platform of twigs, attached to a central axis. On either surface of the platform was fastened a large piece of putrid venison, with other matters by no means pleasant to my olfactory nerves, although no doubt attractive to the Wolves. My companion wished to visit them that evening, merely as he was in the habit of doing so daily, for the purpose of seeing that all was right. He said that Wolves were very abundant that autumn, and had killed nearly the whole of his sheep and one of his colts, but that he was now "paying them off in full," and added that if I would tarry a few hours with him next morning, he would beyond a doubt shew me some sport rarely seen in those parts. We retired to rest in due time, and were up with the dawn.

"I think," said my host, "that all's right, for I see the dogs are anxious to get away to the pits, and although they are nothing but curs, their noses are none the worse for that." As he took up his gun, an axe and a large knife, the dogs began to howl and bark, and whisked around us, as if full of joy. When we reached the first pit, we found the bait all gone, and the platform much injured; but the animal that had been entrapped had scraped a subterranean passage for himself and so escaped. On peeping into the next, he assured me that "three famous fellows were safe enough" in it. I also peeped in and saw the Wolves, two black, and the other brindled, all of goodly size, sure enough. They lay flat on the earth, their ears laid close over the head, their eyes indicating fear more than anger. "But how are we to get them out?"—"How, sir," said the farmer, "why by going down to be sure, and ham-stringing them." Being a novice in these matters, I begged to be merely a looker-on. "With all my heart," quoth the farmer, "stand here, and look at me through the brush." Whereupon he glided down, taking with him his axe and knife, and leaving his rifle to my care. I was not a little surprised to see the cowardice of the Wolves. He pulled out successively their hind legs, and with a side stroke of the knife cut the principal tendon above the joint, exhibiting as little fear as if he had been marking lambs.

"Lo!" exclaimed the farmer, when he had got out, "we have forgot the rope; I'll go after it." Off he went accordingly, with as much alacrity as any youngster could shew. In a short time he returned out of breath, and wiping his forehead with the back of his hand. "Now for it." I was desired to raise and hold the platform on its central balance, whilst he, with all the dexterity of an Indian, threw a noose over the neck of one of the Wolves. We hauled it up motionless with fright, as if dead, its disabled legs swinging to and fro, its jaws wide open, and the gurgle in its throat alone indicating that it was alive. Letting him drop on the

ground, the farmer loosened the rope by means of a stick, and left him to the dogs, all of which set upon him with great fury and soon worried him to death. The second was dealt with in the same manner; but the third, which was probably the oldest, as it was the blackest, shewed some spirit, the moment it was left loose to the mercy of the curs. This Wolf, which we afterwards found to be a female, scuffled along on its forelegs at a surprising rate, giving a snap every now and then to the nearest dog, which went off howling dismally with a mouthful of skin torn from its side. And so well did the furious beast defend itself that, apprehensive of its escape, the farmer levelled his rifle at it, and shot it through the heart, on which the curs rushed upon it, and satiated their vengeance on the destroyer of their master's flock.*

* One of the episodes in Audubon's *Ornithological Biography,* Edinburgh, 1835, III, 338–341.

Possum-Hunting in Alabama

PHILIP HENRY GOSSE

An old-fashioned possum hunt, a lowly sport long associated in folklore and myth with the Southern scene and its Negro denizens, is recorded in this narrative. Its author was Philip Henry Gosse (1810–1888), an English zoologist and the father of a celebrated literary critic, Edmund Gosse. At the age of seventeen Gosse, père, migrated to Newfoundland and remained in Canada for a decade or so before trying his luck in the United States. In 1838 he settled for eight months in Dallas County, Alabama, before recrossing the Atlantic for good. In Alabama he supported himself by teaching school in a log cabin situated in a forest, and employed his leisure time by writing letters describing his environs and especially the birds, animals, and insects in the neighborhood. These were first published in a British magazine called *The Home Friend*, and in 1859 were assembled in a book entitled *Letters from Alabama (U.S.), Chiefly Relating to Natural History*. Gosse, himself, professed to be no huntsman, but he described his dozen pupils as all addicts, who handled the long rifle with greater ease than they managed the goosequill and knew more about "twisting a rabbit" out of its hole than they did about conjugating verbs.

I was out last night 'Possum-hunting, and snatch an early hour this morning to describe to you the important affair, amusing enough, certainly, if not very profitable. For several days past, the "niggers," on bringing in the daily cart-load of water-melons for house-consumption, have been loud in complaints of the robberies committed by the "Possums"; and though it would be perfectly competent for these sable gentlemen to impute to Mr. 'Possum their own delinquencies, the value of a water-melon is scarcely a sufficient inducement even for a negro to lie and thieve, seeing that he has abundantly more than he can devour in his own patch, and those, in all probability, finer and better grown than "mas'r's." The report was therefore received with all due credit, and an expedition against the 'Possums was resolved on as soon as the *vis inertiae* could be overcome.

By the aid of my persuasions this consummation was achieved last evening, and we determined on a sally.

As soon as field-work was done, and supper swallowed, preparations commenced. The overseer blew his horn to call such of the hands as were within hearing, out of whom some half-a-dozen were selected, nothing loth; for Sambo likes the wild excitement of a hunt, especially by night, as well as his betters, and enters into it with as much zeal and zest. One or two were set to saddle the horses, others to collect the dogs of the establishment, and others to search up axes for felling trees, knives for clearing away tangled briers in the woods, and a few other small implements, while another was sent into the swamp to procure a dozen pine-knots for torches. Meanwhile the overseer was busy with lead, ladle, and bullet-mould, at the smithy fire, casting ball for the rifles. These preliminaries disposed of an hour or more; there was no hurry, for it would have been useless to go out until night was well commenced, as it was desirable to allow the depredators full time to issue from their retreats, and begin their nocturnal business in the melon-patches.

About half-past nine, then, we set out, a goodly and picturesque cavalcade. There was, first, my worthy host, Major Kendrick, a stout sun-burnt fellow of six feet two, as erect as a sundial, grizzled a little with the labours of some sixty years in the back woods of Georgia, but still hale and strong, with as keen an eye for a wild-cat or a 'coon as the stalwart nephews by his side. His attire would be deemed peculiar with you, though here it is the approved thing. A Panama hat made of the leaves of the palmetto, split fine, low in the crown, and very broad in the flap; a "hunting shirt," or frock, of pink-striped gingham, open all down the front, but girded with a belt of the same; the neck, which is wide and open, is bordered with a frill, which lies upon the shoulders;

loose trowsers, of no describable colour, pattern, or material; short cotton socks, and stout half-boots, of domestic manufacture. Such is the costume of our "king of men," and all the rest of us approach as near to it as we may.

But who are "the rest of us?" Why, the two strapping youths, who call the planter uncle, Zachariah and Bill, each emulous of his patron's stature and accomplishments; Jones, the overseer, a wiry fellow, originally from the far east (Connecticut, I believe), but grown a southerner by a dozen years' experience in negro-driving; and the humble individual who pens these lines, who begins at length to be known by his proper name, instead of "the stranger." We five were mounted on very capital steeds, and behind and around us marched on foot our sable ministers.

It was a lovely night. The sky, almost cloudless, had a depth of tint that was rather purple than blue; and the moon, near the full, was already approaching the zenith. A gentle breeze, warm and balmy, breathed in the summits of the trees, and wafted to us the delicate perfumes from leaf, flower, and fruit, from gum and balsam, with which the night air is commonly loaded. Bright as was the night, however, it was thought requisite to have artificial light, especially as we should have to explore some tall woods, whose gloomy recesses the moon's beams were quite insufficient to illuminate. The knots of the pitch-pine answer admirably for torches, being full of resin, and maintaining a brilliant flame for an hour or more. The glare of broad red light which these flambeaux cast on the leafy walls along which we rode, and the beautiful effect produced on the surrounding shrubs and intervening trees, when the torchbearers passed through some narrow belt of wood, or explored some little grove, was highly novel and picturesque; the flames, seen through the chequering leaves, played and twinkled, and ever and anon frightened a troop of little birds from their roost, and illuminated their plumage as they fluttered by.

At length we reached the melon-patch, and having dismounted and tied our horses to the hanging twigs of the roadside trees, we crossed the rail-fence to beat the ground on foot. It was a large field, entirely covered with melons, the long stems of which trailed over the soft earth, concealing it with the coarse foliage and the great yellow flowers of the

plant; while the fruit, of all sizes, lay about in boundless profusion, from the berry just formed, to the fully matured and already rotten-ripe melon, as large as a butter-firkin. Abundant evidences were visible of the depredations of our game, for numbers of fine ripe melons lay about with large cavities scooped out of them, some showing by their freshness and cleanness that they had been only just attacked, while others were partially dried and discoloured by the burning sun. Moths of various species were collected around the wounded fruit, some of them (which I should have prized for my cabinet, if I had had time and means to capture and bring them home) inert and bloated with the juices which they had been sucking; others fluttering by scores around, or attracted by the light to dance round the torches.

The party had dispersed. I accompanied the planter to the edge of a wood at one side of the patch, while the young men took up similar stations at some distance. The object was to intercept the vermin in their retreat, as, on being alarmed from their repast, they at once make for their fastness in the lofty trees. A negro with his pine-knot stood at each station, illuminating the hoary trunks of the great trees.

Meanwhile the other servants were scouring the field with the dogs, shouting and making as much noise as possible. Again the twinkling lights looked beautiful, and the sound of the negroes' sonorous voices, raised in prolonged shouts with musical cadences, and now and then a snatch of a rattling song, the favourite burden being how a "big racoon" was seen—

". . . . a sittin' on a rail,"

fell very pleasantly on the ear. Occasionally the barking of the curs gave token that game was started; and, presently, the approach of the sound towards us was followed by what looked to be a white cat scampering towards the very chestnut-tree before us, closely pursued by one of the mongrel curs. My friend's fatal rifle turned the creature over as soon as seen; but the very next instant another appeared, and scrambling up the fissured trunk, made good its retreat among the branches.

In the course of an hour another was shot, one was caught and worried by the dogs, and some half-a-dozen others were just glimpsed as they scuttled past us, the light for an instant revealing their grey bodies, but too briefly to allow an aim. We heard, by the reports of our distant friends' rifles, that they had their share of success; and when we assembled at the edge of the field, half-a-dozen Opossums and a Racoon were thrown across the crupper of one of the beasts. The appearance of the latter had been curiously in accordance with the negroes' song; for one of the young men creeping quietly along the fence, had seen the furry gentleman "sittin' on a rail," and looking with outstretched neck and absorbed attention into the field, wondering, doubtless, what all the uproar was about. His senses were not so locked, however, as not to be aroused by the gentle footfall of our young friend; before he could raise his rifle, the Racoon had leaped from the fence, and scoured up an immense sycamore. It seemed a hopeless case; but young Zachariah, vexed at being done by a 'coon, continued to peer up into the tree, hoping that he might get another glance of the animal. Familiar with the habits of the wild denizens of the woods, the youth directed his patient searching gaze to the bases of the great boughs, well knowing that in the fork of one of these the wily creature would seek shelter. At last, he saw against the light of the moon, what seemed the head of the Racoon projecting from one of the greater forks, and steadily watching it, distinctly saw it move. The fatal ball instantly sped, and down came the creature, heavily plumping on the ground.

I had seen Racoons before, yet I looked at the carcase with interest. You probably are aware that it is an animal about as large as a fox, to which it bears some resemblance. It seems, however, larger, from the fullness of its thick and soft fur, and is more heavy-bodied. Its grey coat, black and white face, and bushy tail, alternately banded with black and light grey, entitle it to admiration; while the Opossum, clothed in rough wiry hair, of a dirty greyish white hue, with a long rat-like naked tail, is anything but prepossessing.

The torches were extinguished, and we sauntered slowly home, my friend the planter amusing me by relating a favourite legend to the glory of one Major Scott, who seems in these parts to be the very "Magnus Apollo" of rifle-shooting. It was to this effect:—An old he-racoon had made himself somewhat notorious by his depredations in the poultry-yards, and by his successful stratagems to evade punishment. His favourite fastness was in the topmost boughs of a very lofty sycamore, beyond rifle-reach. One day, a certain Colonel Sharp, who vaunted his skill as a rifleman rather strongly, went out expressly to bring down this same Racoon. The wily rogue, from his impregnable retreat, hearing footsteps, calls out, "Who's there?" "It's I, Colonel Sharp, the smartest shot in all creation, and I'm come out for you." "Oh, ho!" says the 'coon, and, laughing immoderately, begins to play all sorts of pranks, jumping on the boughs, and wagging his tail from side to side, as the unsuccessful shots followed in rapid succession. At length, other footsteps were heard; "Who now?" "It's Major Scott, a lookin' out for 'coons." "O Major! don't waste your powder, I give in; I'm a gone 'coon!" And down he came, and surrendered at discretion.

The Opossum which had been worried by the curs was not by any means dead when we reached the house, and I had an opportunity of witnessing the curious dissimulation which has made the name of this animal proverbial. Though, if left alone for a few moments, the attention of the bystanders apparently diverted from it, it would get on its legs and begin to creep slily away; yet no sooner was an eye turned towards it, than it would crouch up, lie along motionless, with all its limbs supple, as if just dead; nor would any kicks, cuffs, or handlings avail to produce the least token of life, not the opening of an eyelid, or the moving of a foot. There it was, dead, evidently, you would say, if you had not detected it the moment before in the act of stealing off. The initiated, however, can tell a real dead 'Possum from one that is shamming, and the overseer directed my attention to the last joints of the tail. This, during life, is prehensile, used to catch and hold the twigs like a fifth hand; and even in the hypocritical state in which I saw it, the coil of the tail-tip was maintained, whereas in absolute death this would be relaxed permanently. The propriety of correct classification was impressed on me during my examination. I inadvertently spoke of it as "a singular creature"; but *creature,* or rather "critter," is much too honourable a term for such an animal, being appropriated to cattle. The overseer promptly corrected my mistake. "A 'Possum, Sir, is not a critter, but a varmint."*

---

* Philip Henry Gosse, *Letters from Alabama,* London, 1859, pp. 226–234.

A Duck Hunt in Florida

CHARLES E. WHITEHEAD

With its enormous coastline and perfect location with respect to the chief North American flyways, the South has always provided a favorite hunting ground for wildfowl. In bygone days the varieties of birds pursued by huntsmen ranged from robins, woodcock, quail, and passenger pigeons to waterfowl of many sorts. Ducks were prime favorites. Few sportsmen from the North who possessed sufficient means and leisure failed to make at least one journey during the duck season to the Chesapeake or Currituck regions, and many even ventured as far as Florida or Louisiana on yearly junkets. While there were professional guides who arranged camping trips, friends who lived on plantations in suitable areas were most favored as providers of the best opportunities to take a crack at the birds—canvasbacks, mallards, swans, geese, ibis, and many others besides. If the conditions were favorable the flocks of waterfowl that greeted the hunter on a frosty morning in Dixie seemed to be without limit. And there was that old-style Southern hospitality to boot! There is record of a Louisiana planter who provided a boat capable of transporting a dozen horses and two packs of dogs on deck, and equipped with an "elaborately stocked" bar. Appropriately, it was named *Nimrod*.

This tale by Charles Edward Whitehead (1827–1903) illustrates the plentifulness of wildfowl. Its author was a New Yorker who entered the legal profession after graduating from Rutgers in 1847. As a corporation lawyer, Whitehead took an active part in the management of railroads and for years served as president of the New York, Pennsylvania and Rock Island Railroad. His obituary in the New York *Times* made particular mention of one of his proudest boasts, that he had hunted or fished in every state in the Union. The chief monument to his hobby is a book entitled *Wild Sports in the South; or, The Camp-Fires of the Everglades*

(1860), which was fashioned from articles previously published in the *Spirit of the Times,* a prominent New York journal devoted to the turf, sports, and the theater. The book was reprinted in Edinburgh in 1891, at which time a British reviewer observed: "As regards his wood-craft we have not detected a single mistake, although it must be admitted that his shoulder-gun brings down an almost incredible number of ducks at a shot." But, then, the reviewer had to admit also that he had never heard of the Everglades before.

THE Drowned Lands were formed by the sea banking up with a sandbar the outlet of a stream that ran through a low country. This natural dam flooded the lowlands on either side for several miles, and the soil being sandy, with a slight deposit of alluvial matter from the descending fresh waters, many varieties of grass and aquatic plants sprang up, and formed attractive food for the myriads of water-fowl that here passed the winters. Patches of cane grew on the marshy land not yet covered with water. Osiers and rushes sprung from the shallow water, and a long grass, with a tassel like the onion, opened its crown and scattered its oily seeds over the water. Now and then a floating log, or some still living bulb that had come down the stream had taken root in the shallows, and formed an island, on which rose one or two trees, and a rank vegetation of vines and grass. On the dead upper limbs of these trees the anhinga and other species of cormorants could be seen all the day patiently watching for their prey in the shallows. Fancy could not picture a more suitable home for the water-fowl, whose food was abundant in the matted grass and succulent weeds, and who hid in bending rushes for better shelter from the northerly winds.

Up this extended marsh our boats gently floated, each one following the openings that seemed best, and diverging so as to form an extended line. The negroes shipped their long oars, and used only the paddle, in order to move with greater stillness, and to pass through the narrow openings. As we advanced, I soon lost sight of the other boats, but from time to time could tell their position from the report of their guns and the rising of the ducks they disturbed. I had changed positions with the men, taking the bow of the boat, and letting them paddle in the stern.

"Dar, Maussa, black duck!" whispered Scipio, after we had paddled a short distance, changing with a wave of his paddle the direction of the canoe, and pointing it toward a mass of reeds that lay twisted and broken together, as though some wind had twisted them off half way up.

I pointed my hand inquiringly to the reeds. Scipio nodded, and the boat floated up noiselessly as a fish. We were close by them, and no sign of the game, save a feather or two on the water. The neighboring tufts of grass shut out the wind, and it was warm and still, like summer in the grassy bower, while bright little fish darted aside on either bow of the boat. Then came a flopping sound, a rattle of the reeds, and the brazen cry that so many thousand times, in a thousand hearts, has sent the blood leaping with its old memory-haunted tone, "Qua-ack! qua-ack! quack!" Some notes in this world are clearer, and some more rhythmic, but there are few that when repeated, even far away, will so picture to the mind, in the twinkling of an eye, the extended reach of sedge, the downy reeds, glassy water, and young hopes, with which it is so intimately associated.

With the alarm cry two ducks broke forth, scattering the floss of the cat-tails in clouds about them, their long necks stretching out as though straining to be away. I aimed at the drake as he poised himself to bear away, and with the report of the piece he fell, head and wings pendent, with a splash on the water—a dead shot, I knew by the way he came down. The duck had gained some distance by this time, going straight away, as if terror chased her. No fear of her escape; the success of my first shot gave me confidence, and I knew the power of the little Mullen gun I held at my shoulder. Canny John Mullen, in his grim little smithy in Ann street, working away with his brogue and cunning hand—how often I have thanked him when he never knew it! "Quack! quack!" The sound was faint from the distance when I fired, but the duck rolled over and over, with its wings spinning, till it was lost to sight.

"Yah! ha! ya! Maussa; good shot. Did you ebber? Well, now, I give up—dat beats dis child!"

We paddled on, and found the first duck dead, and the second with

both wings broken, and easily secured. While loading, four ducks came flying over from the direction of the other boats. I hastily poured in some loose shot, and crouching down in the canoe, capped my gun, while I watched the birds approach, and when they were so near I could see the mottling on their breasts, arose suddenly to my feet. Scared by my sudden appearance, they breasted the air, swerving off to the right and left. Ho! what fair shots! I could have killed them with a pistol. The first barrel brought two, the second, one, and the other bird departed sadly frightened.

Thus we passed on, getting fair shots every fifty yards at small bunches of ducks that arose from the little lagoons, and an occasional long shot at some passing bird that had been frightened from his proper feeding-ground by the incursion of the hunters.

At the same time that the game was abundant, the scenery through which its pursuit was leading us was strikingly peculiar. The level waste of sedge extended beyond the vision, waving in the wind. The constant opening and closing of watery passages, the little reed-locked lakes, the tortuous course we were obliged to follow, the sameness of the grouping of the reeds and little islets, repeated over and over again till the mind was all afloat as to locality and distance; the weird trees with their dead and naked arms, and the occasional mass of broken reeds and matted drift-wood that in the summer had formed the alligator's lair, all contributed to impress the mind with a feeling of strangeness and solitude. The wild birds, too, were unwontedly familiar in their demeanor. Marsh hens ran over the drifts before the boat, and gulls came screaming around us.

About three miles from where we had entered the Drowned Lands, we came to the edge of open water, and found a large lake. Before entering it a glance ahead showed the further end of the pond literally covered with ducks. It was impossible, being on the same level, to tell how many there were, but from the extent of their front line they were very numerous. A hurried council of war was called to decide how they were best approached, and after two or three plans had been proposed and discarded, it was settled that we should try and paddle around on the further side of the pond so as to be near the flock, and then take our chances of their coming over us, as they probably might when alarmed by the firing in the other boats. So with much care as to the noise we might make, and some self-control in not firing at single ducks that would rise close by us, we ultimately got around the flock, so as to place them between us and the other boats. We pulled our canoe into the thickest of the grass that completely sheltered us, and from where I sat I could see the ducks lying on the open water, moving hither and thither, and diving down for the eel-grass below the surface. I immediately recognized them as the same flock of teal that came over at the early dawn. It was a beautiful thing to see so much graceful life so bountifully supplied and protected by its own instincts in the solitude.

Away down the marsh came the frequent boom! boom! of my comrades' guns, but it did not seem to interfere with the comfort of the ducks, who still fed on, though keeping out of shot from where I sat. Soon the report of the guns coming nearer caused the ducks to crowd together with all their heads up. There was a long pause, and then a negro's voice sounded close by: "Maussa Jackson, mark!" followed by the clear ringing of a double shot, and at the sound up went my flock of ducks. Three or four arose first, and then the whole mass cleared the water; and the beating of their wings on the surface was like a long continued roll of thunder. I had no conception, before they rose, of their great multitude. It seemed as if they could be counted by tens of thousands. When they had attained a sufficient height to overlook the meadow, they wheeled like the line of an army, and apparently catching sight of the other boats, came with the bright linings of their wings turned to the sunlight, and their countless pinions hurtling through the air directly over the place where we were concealed. I had given Scipio, as a reward of merit, the musket I had brought with me, directing him to take his own time, and fire as he chose. He, however, could not wait for the best shot, but fired as one wing of the army wheeled over us. The aim was not a bad one, for a dozen ducks fell at the shot, and several more at intervals came slanting down from the flock. The effect of this unexpected attack drove the wing of the flock into the main body, clustering them together in a compact mass, when I fired both barrels. My stronger shooting gun bored a hole through the black mass, and twenty-seven ducks fell on the open water, and two or three went down aslant into the reeds. Three and a half dozen ducks was the contribution that one flock made to our booty. I still looked longingly after them as they went floating around the horizon, like banks of minute flies that wave at midsummer from prominent points on the shores of great lakes, undulating with the wind. But they passed away in the dim horizon, probably being unwilling to make another trial of the Drowned Lands after so unpleasant a reception.*

* Charles E. Whitehead, *Wild Sports in The South,* New York, 1860, pp. 217–223.

Ibis Shooting in Louisiana

ANONYMOUS

The following account of an adventure in a Louisiana bayou first appeared in 1853 in *Harper's Magazine,* a journal which published a considerable number of hunting stories in its earlier days. Its author is unknown, but his reference to obtaining specimens for mounting and his use of the scientific names for various birds and animals indicate that, perhaps, he was an amateur naturalist. While his story is heightened by conscious stylistic techniques, the substance of his narrative is well within the bounds of probability. Certainly it conveys the atmosphere of the labyrinthine Louisiana swamps.

In the bayous, of course, the water moccasin and the alligator were the animals which attracted the chief attention, because of an exaggerated belief in their threat to human life. But alligators were little hunted, for hunting's sake, before the Civil War. More often than not, they were regarded merely as varmints, and most of them were shot with rifles from boats and pirogues while they floated in the water or were killed while they lay on the banks sunning themselves.

THE ibis (*tantalus*) is one of the most curious and interesting of American birds: it is a creature of the warm climates, and is not found in either the northern or middle States—the tropics, and the countries contiguous to them, are its range. Louisiana, from its low elevation, possesses almost a tropical climate; and the ibis, of several varieties, is to be there met with in considerable numbers.

There are few sorts of game I have not followed with horse, hound, or gun; and, among other sports, I have gone ibis-shooting: it was not so much for the sport, however, as that I wished to obtain some specimens for mounting. An adventure befell me in one of these excursions that may interest the reader. The southern part of the State of Louisiana is one vast labyrinth of swamps, bayous, and lagoons. These bayous are sluggish streams that glide sleepily along, sometimes running one way, and sometimes the very opposite, according to the season. Many of them are outlets of the great Mississippi, which begins to shed off its waters more than three hundred miles from its mouth. These bayous are deep, sometimes narrow, sometimes wide, with islets in their midst. They and their contiguous swamps are the great habitat of the alligator and the fresh-water shark—the gar. Numerous species of water and wading fowl fly over them, and plunge through their dark tide. Here you may see the red flamingo, the egret, the trumpeter-swan, the blue-heron, the wild-goose, the crane, the snake-bird, the pelican, and the ibis; you may likewise see the osprey, and the white-headed eagle robbing him of his prey. These swamps and bayous produce abundantly fish, reptile, and insect, and are, consequently, the favorite resort of hundreds of birds which prey upon these creatures. In some places, the bayous form a complete network over the country, which you may traverse with a small boat in almost any direction; indeed, this is the means by which many settlements communicate with each other. As you approach southward toward the Gulf, you get clear of the timber; and within some fifty miles of the sea there is not a tree to be seen.

It was near the edge of this open country I went ibis-shooting. I had set out from a small French or Creole settlement, with no other company than my gun; even without a dog, as my favorite spaniel had the day before been bitten by an alligator while swimming across a bayou. I went of course in a boat, a light skiff, such as is commonly used by the inhabitants of the country.

Occasionally using the paddles, I allowed myself to float some four or five miles down the main bayou; but as the birds I was in search of did not appear, I struck into a "branch," and sculled myself upstream. This carried me through a solitary region, with marshes stretching as far as the eye could see, covered with tall reeds. There was no habitation, nor aught that betokened the presence of man. It was just possible that I was the first human being who had ever found a motive for propelling a boat through the dark waters of this solitary stream. As I advanced, I fell in with my game; and I succeeded in bagging several, both of the great wood-ibis and the white species. I also shot a fine white-headed eagle (*Falco leucocephalus*), which came soaring over my boat, unconscious of danger. But the bird which I most wanted seemed that which could not be obtained. I wanted the scarlet ibis.

I think I had rowed some three miles upstream, and was about to take in my oars and leave my boat to float back again, when I perceived that, a little further up, the bayou widened. Curiosity prompted me to continue; and after pulling a few hundred strokes further, I found myself at the end of an oblong lake, a mile or so in length. It was deep, dark, marshy around the shores, and full of alligators. I saw their ugly forms and long serrated backs, as they floated about in all parts of it, hungrily hunting for fish, and eating one another; but all this was nothing new, for I had witnessed similar scenes during the whole of my excursion. What drew my attention most was a small islet near the middle of the lake, upon one end of which stood a row of upright forms of a bright scarlet color: these red creatures were the very objects I was in search of. They might be flamingoes: I could not tell at that distance. So much the better, if I could only succeed in getting a shot at them; but these creatures are even more wary than the ibis; and as the islet was low, and altogether without cover, it was not likely they would allow me to come within range; nevertheless, I was determined to make the attempt. I rowed up the lake, occasionally turning my head to see if the game had taken the alarm. The sun was hot and dazzling; and as the bright scarlet was magnified by refraction, I fancied for a long time they were flamingoes. This fancy was dissipated as I drew near. The outlines of the bills, like the blade of a sabre, convinced me they were the ibis; besides, I now saw that they were only about three feet in height, while the flamingoes stand five feet. There were a dozen of them in all. These were balancing themselves, as is their usual habit, on one leg, apparently asleep, or *buried in deep thought.* They were on the upper extremity of the islet, while I was approaching it from below. It was not above sixty yards across; and could I only reach the point nearest me, I knew my gun would throw shot to kill at that distance. I feared the stroke of

the sculls would start them, and I pulled slowly and cautiously. Perhaps the great heat—for it was as hot a day as I can remember—had rendered them torpid or lazy. Whether or not, they sat still until the cut-water of my skiff touched the bank of the islet. I drew my gun up cautiously, took aim, and fired both barrels almost simultaneously. When the smoke cleared out of my eyes, I saw that all the birds had flown off except one that lay stretched out by the edge of the water. Gun in hand, I leaped out of the boat, and ran across the islet to bag my game. This occupied but a few minutes; and I was turning to go back to the skiff, when, to my consternation, I saw it out upon the lake, and rapidly floating downward! In my haste I had left it unfastened, and the bayou current had carried it off. It was still but a hundred yards off, but it might as well have been a hundred miles, for at that time I could not swim a stroke.

My first impulse was to rush down to the lake, and after the boat; this impulse was checked on arriving at the water's edge, which I saw at a glance was fathoms in depth. Quick reflection told me that the boat was gone—irrecoverably gone!

I did not at first comprehend the full peril of my situation; nor will you. I was on an islet, in a lake, only half a mile from its shores—alone, it is true, and without a boat; but what of that? Many a man had been so before, with not an idea of danger. These were first thoughts, natural enough; but they rapidly gave place to others of a far different character. When I gazed after my boat, now beyond recovery—when I looked around, and saw that the lake lay in the middle of an interminable swamp, the shores of which, even could I have reached them, did not seem to promise me footing—when I reflected that, being unable to swim, I could not reach them—that upon the islet there was neither tree, nor log, nor bush; not a stick out of which I might make a raft—I say, when I reflected upon all these things, there arose in my mind a feeling of well-defined and absolute horror.

It is true, I was only in a lake, a mile or so in width; but so far as the peril and helplessness of my situation were concerned, I might as well have been upon a rock in the middle of the Atlantic. I knew that there was no settlement within miles—miles of pathless swamp. I knew that no one could either see or hear me—no one was at all likely to come near the lake; indeed I felt satisfied that my faithless boat was the first keel that had ever cut its waters. The very tameness of the birds wheeling around my head was evidence of this. I felt satisfied, too, that without someone to help me, I should never go out from that lake: I must die on the islet, or drown in attempting to leave it.

These reflections rolled rapidly over my startled soul. The facts were clear, the hypothesis definite, the sequence certain; there was no ambiguity, no supposititious hinge upon which I could hang a hope; no, not one. I could not even expect that I should be missed and sought for: there was no one to search for me. The simple *habitans* of the village I had left knew me not—I was a stranger among them; they only knew me as a stranger, and fancied me a strange individual; one who made lonely excursions, and brought home bunches of weeds, with birds, insects, and reptiles which they had never before seen, although gathered at their own doors. My absence, besides, would be nothing new to them, even though it lasted for days: I had often been absent before, a week at a time. There was no hope of my being missed.

I have said that these reflections came and passed quickly. In less than a minute my affrighted soul was in full possession of them and almost yielded itself to despair. I shouted, but rather involuntarily than with any hope that I should be heard; I shouted loudly and fiercely: my answer—the echoes of my own voice, the shriek of the osprey, and the maniac laugh of the white-headed eagle.

I ceased to shout, threw my gun to the earth, and tottered down beside it. I have been in a gloomy prison, in the hands of vengeful guerilla banditti, with carbines cocked to blow out my brains. No one will call that a pleasant situation—nor was it so to me. I have been lost upon the wide prairie—the land-sea—without bush, break, or star to guide me—that was worse. There you look around; you see nothing; you hear nothing: you are alone with God, and you tremble in his presence; your senses swim; your brain reels; you are afraid of yourself; you are afraid of your own mind. Deserted by everything else, you dread lest it, too, may forsake you. There is horror in this—it is very horrible—it is hard to bear; but I have borne it all, and would bear it again twenty times over rather than endure once more the first hour I spent on that lonely islet in that lonely lake. Your prison may be dark and silent, but you feel that you are not utterly alone; beings like yourself are near, though they may be your jailers. Lost on the prairie, you are alone; but you are free. In the islet, I felt that I was alone; that I was not free: in the islet, I experienced the feelings of the prairie and the prison combined.

I lay in a state of stupor—almost unconscious; how long I know not, but many hours I am certain: I knew this by the sun—it was going down when I awoke, if I may so term the recovery of my stricken senses. I was aroused by a strange circumstance: I was surrounded by dark objects of hideous shape and hue—reptiles they were. They had been before my eyes for some time, but I had not seen them. I had only a sort of dreamy consciousness of their presence; but I heard them at length: my ear was in better tune, and the strange noises they uttered reached my intellect. It sounded like the blowing of great bellows, with now and then a note harsher and louder, like the roaring of a bull. This startled me, and I looked up and bent my eyes upon the objects: they were forms of the *crocodilidae,* the giant lizards—they were alligators.

Huge ones they were, many of them; and many were they in number—a hundred at least were crawling over the islet, before, behind, and on all sides around me. Their long gaunt jaws and channeled snouts projected forward so as almost to touch my body; and their eyes, usually leaden, seemed now to glare.

Impelled by this new danger, I sprang to my feet, when, recognizing the upright form of man, the reptiles scuttled off, and plunging hurriedly into the lake, hid their hideous bodies under the water.

The incident in some measure revived me. I saw that I was not alone; there was company even in the crocodiles. I gradually became more myself; and began to reflect with some degree of coolness on the circumstances that surrounded me. My eyes wandered over the islet; every inch of it came under my glance; every object upon it was scrutinized—the moulted feathers of wild-fowl, the pieces of mud, the fresh-water mussels (*unios*) strewed upon its beach—all were examined. Still the barren answer—no means of escape.

The islet was but the head of a sand-bar, formed by the eddy—perhaps gathered together within the year. It was bare of herbage, with the exception of a few tufts of grass. There was neither tree nor bush upon it—not a stick. A raft indeed! There was not wood enough to make a raft that would have floated a frog. The idea of a raft was but briefly entertained; such a thought had certainly crossed my mind, but a single glance round the islet dispelled it before it had taken shape.

I paced my prison from end to end; from side to side I walked it over. I tried the water's depth; on all sides I sounded it, wading recklessly in; everywhere it deepened rapidly as I advanced. Three lengths of myself from the islet's edge, and I was up to my neck. The huge reptiles swam around, snorting and blowing; they were bolder in this element. I could not have waded safely ashore, even had the water been shallow. To swim it—no—even though I swam like a duck, they would have closed upon and quartered me before I could have made a dozen strokes. Horrified by their demonstrations, I hurried back upon dry ground, and paced the islet with dripping garments.

I continued walking until night, which gathered around me dark and dismal. With night came new voices—the hideous voices of the nocturnal swamp; the qua-qua of the night-heron, the screech of the swamp-owl, the cry of the bittern, the el-l-uk of the great water-toad, the tinkling of the bell-frog, and the chirp of the savanna-cricket—all fell upon my ear. Sounds still harsher and more hideous were heard around me—the plashing of the alligator, and the roaring of his voice; these reminded me that I must not go to sleep. To sleep! I durst not have slept for a single instant. Even when I lay for a few minutes motionless, the dark reptiles came crawling round me—so close that I could have put forth my hands and touched them.

At intervals, I sprang to my feet, shouted, swept my gun around, and chased them back to the water, into which they betook themselves with a sullen plunge, but with little semblance of fear. At each fresh demonstration on my part they showed less alarm, until I could no longer drive them either with shouts or threatening gestures. They only retreated a few feet, forming an irregular circle round me. Thus hemmed in, I became frightened in turn. I loaded my gun and fired: I killed none. They are impervious to a bullet, except in the eye, or under the forearm. It was too dark to aim at these parts; and my shots glanced harmlessly from the pyramidal scales of their bodies. The loud report, however, and the blaze frightened them, and they fled, to return again after a long

interval. I was asleep when they returned; I had gone to sleep in spite of my efforts to keep awake. I was startled by the touch of something cold and half-stifled by a strong musky odor that filled the air. I threw out my arms; my fingers rested upon an object slippery and clammy: it was one of those monsters—one of gigantic size. He had crawled close alongside me, and was preparing to make his attack; as I saw that he was bent in the form of a bow, and I knew that these creatures assume that attitude when about to strike their victim. I was just in time to spring aside, and avoid the stroke of his powerful tail, that the next moment swept the ground where I had lain. Again I fired, and he with the rest once more retreated to the lake.

All thoughts of going to sleep were at an end. Not that I felt wakeful; on the contrary, wearied with my day's exertion—for I had had a long pull under a hot tropical sun—I could have lain down upon the earth, in the mud, anywhere, and slept in an instant. Nothing but the dread certainty of my peril kept me awake. Once again before morning, I was compelled to battle with the hideous reptiles, and chase them away with a shot from my gun.

Morning came at length, but with it no change in my perilous position. The light only showed me my island prison, but revealed no way of escape from it. Indeed, the change could not be called for the better, for the fervid rays of an almost vertical sun burned down upon me until my skin blistered. I was already speckled by the bites of a thousand swamp-flies and musquitoes, that all night long had preyed upon me. There was not a cloud in the heavens to shade me; and the sunbeams smote the surface of the dead bayou with a double intensity. Toward evening I began to hunger; no wonder at that: I had not eaten since leaving the village settlement. To assuage thirst, I drank the water of the lake, turbid and slimy as it was. I drank it in large quantities, for it was hot, and only moistened my palate without quenching the craving of my appetite. Of water there was enough; I had more to fear from want of food.

What could I eat? The ibis. But how to cook it? There was nothing wherewith to make a fire—not a stick. No matter for that. Cooking is a modern invention, a luxury for pampered palates. I divested the ibis of its brilliant plumage, and ate it raw. I spoiled my specimen, but at the time there was little thought of that: there was not much of the naturalist left in me. I anathematized the hour I had ever imbibed such a taste; I wished Audubon, and Buffon, and Cuvier up to their necks in a swamp. The ibis did not weigh above three pounds, bones and all. It served me for a second meal, a breakfast; but at this *déjeuner sans fourchette* I picked the bones.

What next! Starve? No—not yet. In the battles I had had with the alligators on the second night, one of them had received a shot that proved mortal. The hideous carcass of the reptile lay dead upon the beach. I need not starve; I could eat that. Such were my reflections. I must hunger, though, before I could bring myself to touch the musky morsel. Two more days' fasting conquered my squeamishness. I drew out my knife, cut a steak from the alligator's tail, and ate it—not the one I had first killed, but a second; the other was now putrid, rapidly decomposing under the hot sun: its odor filled the islet.

The stench had grown intolerable. There was not a breath of air stirring; otherwise I might have shunned it by keeping to windward. The whole atmosphere of the islet, as well as a large circle around it, was impregnated with the fearful effluvium. I could bear it no longer. With the aid of my gun, I pushed the half-decomposed carcass into the lake; perhaps the current might carry it away. It did: I had the gratification to see it float away. This circumstance led me into a train of reflections. Why did the body of the alligator float? It was swollen—inflated with gases. Ha!

An idea shot suddenly through my mind, one of those brilliant ideas—the children of necessity. I thought of the floating alligator, of its intestines—what if I inflated them? Yes, yes! buoys and bladders, floats and life-preservers! that was the thought. I would open the alligators, make a buoy of their intestines, and that would bear me from the islet!

I did not lose a moment's time; I was full of energy: hope had given me new life. My gun was loaded—a huge crocodile that swam near the shore received the shot in his eye. I dragged him on the beach; with my knife I laid open his entrails. Few they were, but enough for my purpose. A plume-quill from the wing of the ibis served me for a blow-pipe. I saw the bladder-like skin expand, until I was surrounded by objects like great sausages. These were tied together and fastened to my body, and then, with a plunge, I entered the waters of the lake, and floated downward. I had tied my life-preservers in such a way that I sat in the water in an upright position, holding my gun with both hands. This I intended to have used as a club in case I should be attacked by the alligators; but I had chosen the hot hour of noon, when these creatures lie in a half-torpid state, and to my joy I was not molested. Half an hour's drifting with the current carried me to the end of the lake, and I found myself at the debouchure of the bayou. Here, to my great delight, I saw my boat in the swamp, where it had been caught and held fast by the sedges. A few minutes more, and I had swung myself over the gunwale, and was sculling with eager strokes down the smooth waters of the bayou.*

* *Harper's New Monthly Magazine,* VII, 768-772 (Nov., 1853).

Woodcock Fire-Hunting

THOMAS BANGS THORPE

According to the best poetical tradition, the hunter's heart was supposed to rejoice in the highlands, but in the Old South the swamplands contributed even more to the sportsman's joys. There the abundance of game was as remarkable as the methods sometimes employed in pursuing it. This and the succeeding selection provide two illustrations.

The first was written by Thomas Bangs Thorpe (1815–1878), New England born but a New Yorker by adoption, who left college because of poor health and in 1839 moved down to Louisiana to recuperate. He had been briefly trained as a painter and at first undertook to pay his way by going from plantation to plantation to make portraits of the wealthy gentry and their families. It did not take him long to find out that life in the backwoods was picturesque and that he possessed a natural affinity for the pleasures of the hunt. When painting portraits failed to support him sufficiently, Thorpe turned to newspaper journalism, in New Orleans as well as in lesser cities, and, encouraged by his new Southern friends, began submitting sketches of local characters to a leading New York periodical devoted to hunting and the turf. "Tom Owen, the Bee-Hunter" was the first. A later sketch, of the tall-tale order, entitled "The Big Bear of Arkansas" (1841) carried his fame all over the country and has been frequently reprinted as a celebrated example of early humor of the "frontier" type. His biography has been well delineated by Milton Rickels in *Thomas Bangs Thorpe: Humorist of the Old Southwest* (Baton Rouge, 1962).

Thorpe is now regarded as one of the founders of the "Southwestern" school of humorists. While his consequence as a "funny fellow" is not to be disparaged, it should be remarked that a considerable store of his sketches was meant to provide faithful depictions of life in the backwoods, especially rural sports. Indeed, the number of Thorpe's accounts of hunting that bear the earmarks of an authentic record is actually larger than his writings of the tall-tale order. The following selection, on hunting woodcock, is an example. It appeared in the *Spirit of the Times* for May 1, 1841, and was soon reprinted both in London and New York.

ONE of the most beautiful and "legitimate" amusements of gentlemen is woodcock shooting. In the "backwoods," where game of every kind is plentiful, it is pursued as often as a necessary of life as for the gratification afforded by the sport.

Persons living in the hotbeds of civilization, but who yet retain enough of the old leaven of the wild man to love to destroy the birds of the air, and the beasts of the field, are obliged to eke out the excitements of the field by conventional rules, which prescribe the manner of killing, the weapon to be used, and the kind of dog to be employed;—and the sportsman who is most correct in all these named particulars is deservedly a "celebrity" in his day and generation.

No sport is more properly guarded and understood by amateur hunters than woodcock shooting, and no sport is more esteemed. Therefore, it was that the announcement that there was a section of the United States where the game bird was hunted by torchlight, and killed "without the benefit of clergy," created the same sensation among the "legitimists," as is felt at Saint Germain's, because there is "no Bourbon on the throne"—a thrill of horror pervaded the hearts of many who could believe such a thing *possible*—while the more "strait laced" and deeply conscientious, disbelieved entirely, and pronounced the report too incredible for anything but a "hoax." Yet, woodcock fire-hunting is a fact, although most circumscribed in its geographical limits, the reasons for which will appear in the attempt at a description of the sport.

Woodcock fire-hunting is almost entirely confined to a narrow strip of country running from the mouth of the Mississippi, up the river about three hundred miles. This narrow strip of country is the rich and thickly settled land that borders on the river, and which varies from one to three miles in width; it is in fact nothing but the ridge or high ground that separates the Mississippi from the interminable swamps that compose so great a portion of the State of Louisiana.

The habits of the woodcock made it entirely a nocturnal bird; it retires into these swamps that border its feeding grounds during the day, and is perfectly safe from interruption; hidden among the tangled vines, cane-brakes, and boggy land, it consults alike its pleasure and safety; finds convenient places for its nests, and raises its young, with the assurance of being undisturbed. As a matter of course they increase rapidly, until these solitudes become alive with their simple murmuring note; and when evening sets in, they fill the high land which we have described in numbers which can scarcely be imagined by anyone except an eye-witness.

Another cause, probably, of their being so numerous in this section of the country may be owing to their migratory habits, as the bird is seen as far north as the river St. Lawrence in summer, and we presume that these very birds return for their winter residence in Louisiana in the very months when "fire-hunting" is practiced, which is in the latter part of December, January, and the first part of February.

Yet, a resident in the vicinity or among the haunts of these birds, may live a life through, and make day hunting a business, yet be unconscious that woodcock inhabit his path; so much is this the case, that I do not know of the birds ever being hunted, in the common and universal way, in the places where fire-hunting them is practiced.

This novel sport, we presume, originated among the descendants of the French, who originally settled on the whole tract of country bordering on the Mississippi, as high up as it favors this kind of sport. Here it is, that "Beccasse" forms a common dish when in season, in which the poor and the wealthy indulge as a luxury, too common to be a variety, and too excellent not to be always welcome.

With these preliminaries let us prepare for the sport.

Provide yourself with a short double-barrelled fowling-piece of small bore; let your ammunition be first-rate, and have something the size of a small thimble wherewith to measure out your load of mustard shot. Let your powder be in a small flask, but keep your shot loose with your measure, in the right side pocket of your shooting jacket—and, aston-

116 HUNTING IN THE OLD SOUTH

ished sportsman! leave thy noble brace of dogs shut up in their kennels; for we would hunt woodcock, incredible as it may seem, without them.

In the place of the dogs we will put a stout negro, who understands his business, burdened with what resembles an old-fashioned warming-pan, but the bottom, instead of the top, pierced with holes; in this pan are small splinters of pine knot, and we denominate this, the Torch. Then put on the broad-brimmed palmetto hat, so that it will shade your

eyes, and keep them from alarming the birds. Now, follow me down into any of the old fields that lie between the river and the swamp, while the ladies can stand upon spacious galleries that surround the house, and tell by the quick report of guns our success; the streaming light from "the torch," will, to them, from the distance, look like an ignis fatuus dancing the cachuca in the old field.

It is in the middle of January, the night is a favorable one, the weather rather warm, the thermometer says "temperate," and the fog rolls off the cold water into the river like steam; an old "fire-hunter" says, "this is just the night."

Whiz—whiz—hallo! What's here? Sambo, strike a light, and hoist it over your head. Now, friend, place yourself behind the torch, on the left, both of us in the rear to court the shade. Now, torch-bearer, lead on. Whiz—bang—whiz, bang—two woodcock in a minute. Bang, bang. Heavens, this is murder! Don't load too heavy—let your charges be mere squibs, and murder away,—the sport is fairly up.

The birds show plainly from three to ten paces all around you, and you can generally catch them on the ground, but as they rise slowly and perpendicularly from the glare of the light, with a flickering motion, you can bring them down before they start off like arrows into the surrounding darkness. Thank the stars they do not fly many paces before they again alight, so that you can follow the same bird or birds until every one is destroyed. Bang, bang—how exciting—don't the birds look beautiful as they stream up into the light; the slight reddish tinge of their head and breast shining for an instant in the glare of the torch like fire.

Ha! see that stream of gold, bang—and we have a meadow-lark, the bright yellow of its breast being more beautiful than the dull colors of the woodcock. And I see, friend, you have bagged a quail or two. Well, such things occasionally happen. Two hours sport, and we have killed between us nearly thirty birds. With old hunters the average is always more, and a whole night's labor, if successful, is often rewarded with a round hundred.

Practice and experience, as a matter of course, have much to do with success in this sport, but less than in any other; for we have known tyros, on one or two occasions, to do very well with clubs; while the

negroes have threshed them down by "baskets-full" with whips made of bundles of young cane, the birds being so thick that some could be brought down even in this way, while endeavoring, in their confusion, to get out of the glare of the torch.

This fact, and the quantity of birds killed, attest to the extraordinary numbers that inhabit this particular section of country.

Let the birds, however, be less numerous than we have described, and they are on some days more plentiful than on others, and one who is a good shot, in the ordinary way of hunting the bird, has only to overcome his astonishment, and we will add, horror, at the mode in which he sees his favorite game killed, to be a perfect master of woodcock fire-hunting under all circumstances. It is common with those who are fond of sport, and have some sentiment about them, never to fire until the bird rises, and then to bring down a bird with each barrel.

This requires quick shooting, as the torch only sheds an available light in a circle of about twenty yards in diameter. Parties are frequently made up who hunt during a given number of hours, and the destruction of the birds on these occasions is almost beyond belief.

These parties afford rare sport, and are often kept up all night.

When this is the case, the sportsman not unfrequently sleeps to so late an hour in the day that he has only time to rise, sip a cup of strong coffee, and leisurely dress for dinner, when it is announced as ready, and woodcock, plentiful to wasting, are smoking on the board before him.

Such a dinner, the dullest intellect can imagine, is a repast both for sense and soul,—for woodcock and wit are synonymous.*

---

* T. B. Thorpe, *The Hive of "The Bee-Hunter,"* New York, 1854, pp. 225–231.

Deer Hunting in the Yazoo Swamp

YAZOO

The second account of an unusual hunt, which also took place in the Mississippi bottomlands, was sent in to the *Spirit of the Times* as a letter from a subscriber. Who he was it is impossible to say. The classical allusions which pepper his account were fairly commonplace with Southern planters who took up their pens to record their adventures in the field and provide no more grounds for surprise than "Yazoo's" reference to a sumptuous hunt breakfast and the bag of thirty-one deer in five day's hunting.

While the writer considered the method pursued in shooting deer in the Yazoo Swamp as "something of a novelty," it was far from unusual in the low country. Bird dogs were often employed also in the pursuit of deer, and the use of horses in penetrating the thickets was quite common. It was rare, however, for a huntsman to fire at a deer from the saddle. He usually dismounted and tied his horse to a tree before discharging his gun at the quarry.

I wish to communicate to you something of a novelty—it is the manner in which they kill deer in the Yazoo Swamp. I am an old hunter myself—I may say; that is, I have killed deer in various ways, as you shall see, and have had my hand in for the last eighteen or twenty years, having commenced the sport when very young; and with all my experience, I have never before seen that noble animal killed after the fashion which prevails in these diggins; and which I shall attempt to describe.

I have often, when a boy, and at a later period of life too, with my rifle on my shoulder, stalked stealthily through the woods, (generally after a shower of rain, when the fallen leaves would rustle least, and the

small sticks under foot yielded to the tread without cracking), watching with Argus eyes in every direction, until I have come unperceived upon the unsuspecting quarry feeding, and with deadly aim have dropped him in his tracks. I have of a dark night, with a frying-pan upon my shoulder filled with blazing pine knots, sought their haunts, and when their gleaming eye-balls caught my gaze have killed them by dozens. I have in a pirogue, studded round with green boughs for concealment, circumnavigated the small islands in the Mississippi swamp, where the deer have taken refuge in large numbers from the general overflow of the surrounding swamp, and there with my rifle have piled them up in cords! murderous method! I have taken my stand on the points of certain ridges, and while a huntsman with a pack of eager hounds has driven them through, have taken them with my double barrel right and left—on one occasion two at a crack, making them throw sommersaults in the most fantastic style. Fair play this and not to be condemned. So you see, I am no novice in the deer-killing line! Aye; I have taken them at "long taw" in the Texas Prairies but during this long career of slaughter, I have never dreamt of *flushing* them with pointers, and popping them as they 'rose, as you do woodcock and partridges. But this is the way they do things in the Yazoo Swamp.

On the morning of the 25th of February inst., a party who by previous arrangement had met and passed the previous night at the home of a noble South Carolinian—a genuine sportsman both with gun and rod, and a thorough-going "swamper," and

> "Whose hospitable hall is open still,
> To wanderers of the swamp and hill"—

were awakened by a merry blast from a Kent bugle, sounded by the aforesaid swamper. The huntsmen were soon in motion, discharging, wiping and reloading their pieces; and after an early, though sumptuous breakfast, graced by the presence of the beautiful and accomplished lady of our generous host, the order was given "to horse."

Our party consisted of ten, mounted upon the *soberest* hacks the plantation could muster, selected with the view of shooting from their backs without the risk of a fall. One of the party was a Monsieur De____ of Paris, who had crossed the Atlantic in search of savage life, and who had at last found the *Eldorado* of his hopes and wishes in the Yazoo Swamp, and may I not add, the *Pactolus* too, in the noble Yazoo that flowed smoothly by, within fifty feet of where we slept? The Monsieur had never killed a deer, but mounted upon the gentlest horse, and with his highly finished Paris-made gun, he had high hopes of doing something on the present occasion. The cavalcade moved off, Pointers, Terriers, Hounds and all; and after an hour's ride into the bowels of the swamp, it was announced that we had reached the hunting ground. Here we were formed into line by one of the party who knew the localities, and acted as guide, placing each horseman about 40 yards apart; this gave us a front of nearly a quarter of a mile. In this form we would sweep along the palmetto ridges, which are to be found throughout the Swamp, and lie in nearly parallel lines, and where the deer lie concealed during the day, and as they were started from their lair by the horsemen or the dogs, the person nearest them would stop his horse, drop the reins on his neck, level his piece and fire, and generally bring him down. I will here remark that the Yazoo Swamp, although interspersed with thickets, canebrakes, and lakes, is in its general aspect an open wood, free of undergrowth, particularly so on the Palmetto ridges to which I have alluded. These ridges although subject to annual inundation, are some two or three feet above the general level.

Soon after our line was formed and we had fairly entered upon the business of the day, bang!—bang! went two barrels in quick succession on our left. "My liquor," cried the huntsman who had fired;—it was our guide, with a head like Bacchus and a frame like Hercules. "I have drawn the first blood," continued he, "and am entitled to the treat." All awarded it to W⸺ as we rode up and saw the beautiful doe

"Stretch her fleet limbs, to rise no more."

The deer was disemboweled and tied on behind one of the saddles in less than no time; and we are again in motion spreading out as before. Bang!—bang! goes Monsieur's gun, and a noble buck is seen at full speed, passing W⸺ who killed the first deer—he fires, and the forest mourns the loss of another of its denizens. The deer was awarded to Monsieur De⸺ who it was *kindly* alleged had mortally wounded him the second fire; of this, however, there was no evidence, but it was determined that one who had traveled so far for the purpose *should kill a deer,* and it was thought that the present would be the best chance he would get during the day. Very different, however, was the result of the day's sport. Monsieur De____ killed after this two other fine deer without any assistance whatever, and did it, too, in beautiful style. The same process of disembowelling was adopted with each deer, as he was killed. This exciting and to me novel sport we continued for about five hours—riding occasionally several miles without starting any game. Sometimes a deer would be started on the extreme right or left, and run in a direction nearly parallel to our line, just out of range, when every hunter would discharge at him two barrels as he passed, giving the firing the appearance of a *"feu de joie,"* or as termed in the *militaire* "independent file firing."

We killed during this day *seven* fine deer, a wild cat, and two wild turkeys. It is unnecessary for me to inform *you* how we finished the day,—it was highly satisfactory, I assure you. If I recollected the last toast I would give it, but do not.

The same party in five days' hunting, in the way I have described, killed *thirty-one* deer, besides other game.*

---

* *Spirit of the Times,* XIV, 67 (April 6, 1844).

Shooting Extraordinary

X. Y. Z.

John Stuart Skinner (1788–1851), a Marylander and a lawyer by training, in 1829 founded in Baltimore the first important American journal to carry a considerable budget of material on hunting. Entitled the *American Turf Register and Sporting Magazine,* it was dedicated to the improvement of thoroughbred horses and field sports of all kinds. When it was sold ten years later to William T. Porter, its founder remarked that his *Register* "had but one sire and no dam; when it was foaled it was not certain whether it would find food or pasture." Skinner's chief object was to provide a clearinghouse for the history and pedigrees of blooded horses and to record the schedules and results of races. But, as he announced in the first number, natural history, guns, dogs, hunting, and fishing were also to be featured. Skinner was earlier experienced in journalism, and in 1819 had established the *American Farmer,* probably the earliest successful agricultural magazine in the nation. He has another claim to fame that should be mentioned, for it was he who arranged to have "The Star-Spangled Banner" first put into print. Skinner had been a companion of Francis Scott Key during the bombardment of Fort McHenry in September, 1814.

In the first number of the *Register,* the editor encouraged his readers to send in "curious anecdotes" or "interesting facts" dealing with natural history or "rural sports of any kind." A majority of the earliest contributions dealt with hunting and came from the Southern states. Not unnaturally with the horsey set, fox hunting and chasing the deer were favorite topics, but sometimes subscribers sent in letters simply describing their local hunting clubs or merely recording their bags.

When he printed a subscriber's "minutes of a week's hunt" in Dogue Neck, Virginia, Skinner was moved to comment: "Forever confined to the smoke of the city, one must be a stoic who suffers not something of the pains of Tantalus, on reading sketches of sport like that at Dogue's Neck. How can one divest it of the idea of mint juleps in the morning—hominy and canvass backs for breakfast? Dinner—venison, ducks—opossum, ducks—wild turkeys, ducks. At night—whist, ducks, apple toddy—and divers jests about the hunt of the day. . . ."

There was considerable correspondence during the 1830's about the incidence of the red fox in Virginia, and much discussion ensued of the breeds of dogs favored for special purposes. But the most illuminating letters undertook merely to tell a straightforward yarn about a day in the field or, more rarely, to provide a bit of amusement.

Washington, D.C., May, 1830

IN the autumn of 1824, Mr. George Mason, of Gunston, Fairfax County, Va., on the grounds near Alexandria, D.C. belonging to Col. Aug. Smith, killed forty-nine partridges without missing a single shot. Mr. Mason snagged his foot when he first entered the field, and was lame the whole day—he did not fire a gun till after 10 o'clock, and his shot were all expended before sunset, when the birds were most abundant. All the plain shots (that is, when a single bird was pointed close to them in the open field) were given to Lieut. Hamersley, of the Navy, who had just returned from a three years' cruise in the Mediterranean. Mr. M. hunted two pointers, one an imported English dog, and his dog Pluto. The English dog had a high character, was perfectly trained (his owner, Mr. Young, has hired him for the shooting season, at the price of $25). Pluto proved greatly his superior. Although now very old, I believe no dog in Virginia or Maryland can compare with him either for fleetness or staunchness in ranging or finding single birds. Pluto was out of a setter bitch, called Phyllis, who was out of a setter of a breed formerly obtained from Dr. Edward Jones, of the Eastern Shore of Maryland, who, I believe, imported them—and got by Dr. G. Brown's imported Highland setter Bob, one of the best dogs that ever went into a field. Pluto was got by Ponto, who was descended from the first stock of pointers introduced into Virginia. Ponto was a most impetuous dog, and always ran as if he intended to break his neck; yet he never flushed a bird. I once saw him dashing as if the devil was after him, and in the act of springing a high fence, couch suddenly on the top rail, and make a point at a bird *ten or twelve feet above his head, in a tree.* I have often thought I would have given anything for a good painting of his attitude at that moment—except for the intelligence of his eye, he seemed to have been absolutely petrified in a single moment. In reading the accounts of the English sportsmen, it should be borne in mind that the English partridge is larger than ours, more abundant, as the game laws afford them protection, is not so shy, and do not take such rapid flights—of course are easier killed.

The same gentleman killed two bucks, running, at one shot, with a rifle loaded with a single ball. He once shot at eight partridges, flying, and killed them all. He shot at three dippers with a rifle and killed them; struck the two nearest in the head and the other in the neck. I saw him strike a playing card six times running with a pistol, at the distance of thirty yards—the pistol is now in the possession of his brother, Capt. R. B. Mason, of the Army—it poises better and fires with more accuracy than any other in the world—it was made by Prosser, of London. I have frequently seen him take a pistol in each hand, distance ten yards, and in the act of advancing rapidly, strike a lath with each. Mr. Mason shot off the heads of twenty-nine squirrels with his rifle in one day's hunt, in Dogue Neck, without missing one: the last shot was with half a bullet. I have seen him kill hares and foxes, running with a rifle. To kill deer running, with his rifle, and name the place where they were struck, was a thing so common with him that it ceased to excite any surprise. He can throw into the air two apples at once and strike each with a double barrel gun before they fall. I once saw him put a bandage over his eyes so that he could not possibly see, and turn loose ten partridges, one at a time, and kill three at the ten shots. Mr. Mason thinks he can kill one partridge in ten shots (flying) with a rifle—I have no doubt of it myself.

In Charles County, in Maryland, Mr. Mason shot at a paper with a rifle, the paper cut exactly the size of a quarter of a dollar, and struck it four times in succession, the distance sixty yards. Mr. King, one of the gentlemen present, since a member of the Maryland legislature, said it was all chance, accidentally shaking right; but if it could be done with a rest he would be convinced. Mr. M. then laid down, fired from the bank of a ditch, and drove the centre. A paper was then cut out by a five-penny-bit. Mr. M. fired at it thirty yards, with a rest, four times; struck it three times, and missed it the fourth, by about a hair's breadth, owing, he said, to one of the gentlemen speaking to him just as he was touching the trigger. I have seen him drive the centre, a point, three yards, off-hand, five times in succession. I have seen many first-rate rifle shots attempt it without succeeding once in five times—it is more difficult than you would imagine. Mr. Mason killed eighteen white backs at six shots, flying over Hallooing Point, on the Potomac. I saw him kill, with his rifle, three tame pigeons flying, at six shots. I will mention two curious facts, which were related to me by a gentleman now in Tennessee. Mr. M., when a boy, fixed on the top of a cherry tree a dead bush for the cherry birds to light on (every one knows that if there is a dead limb on a tree those birds will always settle on it, as close

as they can cluster), concealed himself behind a blind, with a large duck gun loaded with mustard seed shot—he fired at forty-four and killed them every one. When first learning to shoot, he fired at a hare closely pursued by a dog, missed it, laid down the gun, picked up a stone and killed it.

Yet, with all this extraordinary skill, Mr. Mason had his match, the late Mr. Edgar McCarty, of Fairfax. Mr. McCarty killed three house martins flying with a rifle, and cut the wing feathers of the fourth; when this was mentioned at a barbecue at Dorrel's Spring, Fairfax County; it was doubted by some gentlemen, and ascribed to chance by others. Mr. McCarty offered to bet his saddle horse that he could kill three, in five shots, and Mr. Richard B. Alexander, the gentleman mentioned in your Sporting Magazine, No. 5, page 236, as having killed two deer with one hand, with a double barrel gun, and taking sight at the third, who perfectly knew Mr. McCarty's skill, offered a bet of $100, that Mr. McCarty could do it. Upon inquiry the doubters were convinced, and declined the bets. I have seen Mr. McCarty fire at the bank swallows flying, with a rifle, and strike them so point blank that they would be literally cut to pieces. I could narrate you many more astonishing facts about the skill of these two gentlemen, but I do not choose to risk my character for veracity; however, for several of the facts, and for the extraordinary character they bore as sportsmen, I will refer you to some living witnesses, to wit: Mr. Taliaferro, Member of Congress; Mr. Grymes, Mr. Hooe, and others, of King George County, Va.; Mr. Graham, of the Land Office, Washington; Mr. Lyles and Mr. West, of Md.; Mr. G. Alexander, of Kentucky; Mr. John McCarty and Wm. McCarty, late secretary of the Territory of Florida, both brothers to Mr. Edgar McCarty; *cum multis aliis*. First-rate shots never brag. If ever you hear a bragger; mark him down a junior sportsman, or second-rate. Mr. Mason always said Mr. McCarty was the better shot; Mr. McCarty said the same of Mr. Mason. Take those two gentlemen in the various ways of shooting, with rifles, pistols and shot guns, and their superiors cannot be produced in the whole shooting world. I have often inquired of myself, why they should so excel all other sportsmen, and have come to this conclusion—that to be eminently successful, it requires great presence of mind and great muscular powers. These gentlemen certainly possessed those attributes in a high degree. I have seen them repeatedly try who could strain a horse farthest with a fifty-six pound weight on their head, without its falling off.

Yours
X.Y.Z*

American Turf Register, I, 495–497 (June, 1830).

Hawking in Fairfax, Virginia

M. G.

This next letter to the *American Turf Register* seems to have been written by a Virginia lawyer who followed editor Skinner's suggestion about sending in material of an exceptional sort. Its unique account of an aged clergyman who hunted with hawks certainly departs from the usual run of epistles to the sporting journals. In fact, we may be inclined to doubt that a venerable parson of the Anglican faith would name his horse "Orthodoxy" and his favorite hawks "Death" and "Devil," but on second thought it appears impossible that old Parson Broders was a figment of the imagination. Several subsequent references to Parson Broders in later issues of the *Register* indicate that the readers of the journal assumed him to be a real person.

The writer of the letter comments on the involved terminology associated with hawking, and it must be admitted that he did not always get his terminology straight. The reader will perhaps more willingly pardon the editor for not tampering with the text if he will glance at a handbook on falconry and note the complexity of the technical lingo associated with the ancient sport.

THERE is an old gentleman, the reverend Mr. Broders, in this county, and I expect the only one in any part of America, whose person is constantly attended by those distinguishing companions of a gentleman, the greyhound and the hawk.

The old gentleman sounds the silver trumpet of the gospel on Sundays, courses his greyhounds, or gazehounds, as he calls them, flies his hawks, and kisses a young wife, "charming, chaste, and twenty-three," to whom he is just married, any other day in the week. He is

pious and learned, benevolent and convivial, and is among the last of that band of *"the administrators of the gospel,"* who had the parochial care of our souls before the Revolution—when the church held up her head in Virginia—and at whose houses we always found at least three good things—good wine, good dinners, and family prayers. It would do your heart good to see the venerable old gentleman mounted on his fine horse Orthodoxy, with his hawks, Death and the Devil, on his fist, and his beautiful greyhounds, Romeo and Juliet, by his side. Though seventy years of age, his colloquial powers are unimpaired; his society is much sought after; his conversation instructs the young, and amuses the learned; his literary attainments are great, having received his education at that seat of science, Oxford, in England; his piety, his learning, his benevolence, and his social feelings, make him an universal favourite with young and old. The old gentleman has no objection to betting twenty-five cents, a sum of no great pecuniary magnitude, on a quarter race. If he loses, his serenity is not lost with it—and if he is successful, he boasts of his judgment, and is sure to give his winnings to some ragged urchin on the spot. He plays an excellent hand at whist, and since his marriage, sometimes takes a cut at *all-fours;* but his habits are by no means sedentary.

Hawking is his favourite amusement—the lost privileges of the church, and his own pedigree, his favourite themes. He insists he was descended in a direct line from Thomas à Becket, who he says, was descended from Jean de Brodeau, Duke de Saintonge, who was one of the followers of William the Conqueror. He says: "To be sure Becket was never married, but that only places me in the exact predicament of all the present English nobility." He is devoted to horticultural amusements, and so tastefully is his garden arranged and improved, that the reverend old gentleman says, he should not be surprised if one of these days the descendants of Cain, as Adam's heirs-at-law, should claim his tulip beds as part and parcel of the garden of Eden; and he knows many a lawyer who would take a fee in the case.

I can give you no account of his manner of training his hawks; he is too enveloped in technicals for me to comprehend one word he says on that subject. I don't understand him any more than a plain, common-sense man could his own case in a *court of common law,* on a plain action for debt. "I think, Parson Broders," said I to him the other day, "that Merlin is a finer bird than Devil." "You are mistaken, sir," said he, "Devil is descended from the Goshawks of Puglia; Merlin is a fine bird too; he is from the Tyrone in Ulster. Merlin is a better partridger—but look at the proportions and shape of the Devil—small head, long face, deep set, nares black, pounces large, and she has such force, sir." He then spake of training with jessies and bewets—keeping hawks hooded until they leave off their ramageness—unsealing them always by candle

light, causing them to plume on the leg of a pullet—that they should be creanced at a distance; howet, howet, retrieve a first and second time; mew, and mewtings, &c. &c., all of which was heathen Greek to me.

The reverend gentleman is moreover an excellent archer, having twice won the silver arrow from the Hainault foresters, at the Fairlop Oak, when a student in England; both of which are now in the possession of his son, a distinguished wrangler at the bar of one of our county courts. He frequently makes a cut at his son, the lawyer, by telling him that his are not the only trained hawks in the community; in fact, old Commodore Trunnion never hated those landsharks more than the reverend Mr. Broders. The old gentleman, owing to his education, is High Church and Tory in his principles, and avers, that except the *pa*-rent country (by which name he always calls England), the County of Fairfax can afford the best horses, the best dogs, the most game, the best huntsmen, the best shots, the best fish, the cleverest fellows, and the prettiest girls in all Christendom.

M.G.*

---

* *American Turf Register,* II, 28–29 (Sept., 1830).

Miseries of a Sportsman's Wife

JULIANA ROSEBUD

The jeu d'esprit which follows is not, to be sure, a hunting yarn, but it came to the *Turf Register* in answer to the editor's request for letters from readers. And its subject may still have relevance to present-day experience, though the golf widow is now a more frequent topic of humor than the hunt widow. The piece was, apparently, well liked, for there are a number of references to it in subsequent epistles sent in by subscribers to the journal.

The mention in it of the French horn as part of the hunter's equipment perhaps justifies the reminder that only the sportsmen de luxe were equipped with such instruments. In more elaborate fox hunts, bugles or other metal horns were fairly common, especially in Virginia, but the Southern hunters customarily used the less resonant product of the cow, carried over the shoulder with a string or piece of rawhide.

Rosebud Hall, Fairfax County, Va., 1830

I have naturally the sweetest temper in the world, and two of the most beautiful, as well as the best children, that ever were seen; and should enjoy the bounties which Providence has placed within my reach, if it were not for my husband. The unfeeling wretch is devoted to his dogs, his gun, his horses, his grog, and everything but his wife. We never pass a day without some strife; altogether his fault, as I do not recollect that I ever was in fault in all my life: he provokes me so that I cannot keep my temper. Whenever I assert my rights, he replies: "Mrs. Rosebud, you are the very pink of perfection. I declare, my love, there is an infallibility about you, not to be found in any other woman." Now, Mr. Editor, this is true; but from the manner in which he says it, it is

past endurance. The brute has a great objection to going in debt for anything except powder and shot, and whiskey; yet I am repeatedly telling him, a man's debts are proof of the confidence the public have in him; but he won't believe me. Everybody, too, dislikes my children; though, I declare, they are the sweetest little darlings in all the world. An impudent fellow, the other day, struck up in my presence:

> Two or three girls and two or three boys,
> All ragged and dirty, and making a noise;
> One bawling for this, and one squalling for that;
> One kicking the dog, and one scalding the cat.

My husband had the impudence to laugh; but I soon stopped his mirth, by boxing the songster's ears. My brute most provokingly kept his temper; made me a low bow, and finished, as usual: "I declare, Mrs. Rosebud, you are the very pink of perfection." Now, is not this insufferable? Do, Mr. Editor, write to my husband, and advise him to subscribe to Sunday tracts as well as your Magazine; to change his company of fox hunting friends for decent young ministers of the gospel; his guns and fishing rods for more useful implements, or new furniture. "Do, Mr. Rosebud," said I to him, the other day, "change your French horn, with which you annoy the whole house, for a new piano. Our Juliana, you know, has a fine taste for music, which she gets from me; and you have two or three double-barreled guns, which might be sold to make up the difference." He declared that guns and French horns made better music than pianos. I never was so shocked in all my life. I never have a genteel party but half a dozen rough fox hunters are introduced; and, my last, a very pious young minister of the gospel was nigh breaking his neck over Old Veto, the large pointer dog, which my husband will not suffer to be kicked out of the house. The poor young man, in his vexation, slipt out an oath,* but I don't believe anybody heard him but myself; and I very soon forgave him, he is so sweet and so good.

Do, my dear good Mr. Editor, write to my husband; advise him to give up his fishing boats and his hounds; persuade him to drop his hunting acquaintances, and frequent the society of clergymen, except

---

* He only called the dog *"son of a bitch,"* which is true, you know.

that old fox-hunting parson, Mr. Broders; for I can't bear him. Above all, advise him to send our son Robin, a boy of as fine genius as you ever saw, to the Theological Seminary, and our dear little Juliana to the dancing school, and you will, Mr. Editor, make me everlastingly happy.

JULIANA ROSEBUD*

* *American Turf Register,* II, 339–340 (March, 1831).

Fox Hunt

HAWKEYE

An unknown contributor to the *Turf Register* (whose nom de plume "Hawkeye" no doubt stems from Cooper's renowned Leather-Stocking) provides a dryly humorous account of Southern fox hunting. It is a plain, unvarnished tale of sport in North Carolina, which doubtless had its counterparts in thousands of similar ventures after the reds and the greys in all areas of the South where the ground was open enough to warrant the traditional style of hunting with horses and hounds. This was the kind of sport which George Washington preferred, as his journals amply illustrate. The reference to "Capt. H———r," who could tell of shooting deer on the very spot on which the capitol of the Old North State now stands, likewise provokes an unsatisfied curiosity. But what a symbolic gesture—to choose the site for a state capitol because it was a favorite deer stand! Not the least interesting feature of "Hawkeye's" narrative is his meticulous detail respecting the names and mannerisms of the dogs involved in the hunt.

ON Wednesday last Mr. J. H———d, with several couple of dogs, stopped at my door and told me that the next morning, on his return from his plantation on Swift Creek, he would move upon the deer, any law or usage to the contrary notwithstanding; and that if I could co-operate, his plan of hunting should be in accordance with my convenience and wishes. I told him that the passes upon the Fallen Tree and Rencher's Corner would be occupied at 10 o'clock. He passed on—and soon after, some of my young sporting friends met me, and informed me that a fox chase had been agreed on, and that I was expected to make one of the party; the company to quarter that night with the old sportsman, Capt. H———r, who would take the field, and likewise E. L. and Capt. A. J. The invitation was very acceptable, as the occasion would afford me "a fair field and equal run" with the gentlemen just named, they all like myself being silver greys.

We met at the old cock's agreeably to appointment, held a council, and settled the plan of the hunt. The list of dogs was called over and our calculations noted as follows. W. H——d's dog Damon would be the first to strike. C's Yorrick would lead the pack—my Belmon, though a real skirter, for his wide and rapid circling, would save him upon doublings—and J. H——r's Yellow Rose, upon a long pull would be the sharpest thorn in the side of the fox. E. L's old Rock, with a glove on one of his feet, would take up the dropped stitches, for he would suffer a hundred foxes to escape rather than not put his nose in every identical spot where the fox had trod. Of one-eyed Crazy Kate, we had our hopes and fears. This animal at times is perfectly deranged in mind, supposed to have been produced by the loss of an eye which was torn from its socket while she was making a gallant run. When her crazy fit comes on, though the game may be up, she is just as apt to run the opposite course as any other, and then again when in her right mind, she is all powerful, both on the trail and in the chase. The sympathies of the huntsmen are always interested in behalf of poor Crazy Kate, when she is on the field. No one ever had the heart to be provoked when she did mischief, and she never failed drawing from the huntsmen a loud shout when she did well. Caroline Bell, Speckled Flora, Echo, Juno, Frolic, Jolly, and Jack Falstaff, together with several others not named, were to compose the body of the pack, and relied upon for a fine breast run.

After thus disposing of our forces, the old silver greys, then before a comfortable fire, for their own gratification and for the entertainment of the young sportsmen, fought over the battles of former days. Many a buck was killed—many a long shot was made—many a better dog ran that night than was found in the chase the next day—and many a fox taken in shorter time—many a joke was cracked, and many a good story was told. Capt. H——r could tell of hunts upon the ground on which this *grand city* of Raleigh is built, and what a fine stand for deer was the very spot now occupied by our beautiful capital; and that to this circumstance principally we owe the happy selection of its site. This, Mr. Editor, is an undoubted fact; and were it my purpose to do so, I could establish it to your entire satisfaction but shall leave the task to the historian who may hereafter write the history of the state.

Thus, Mr. Editor, the hours of the evening were beguiled away, till late bedtime, when we were told that, inasmuch as we were beyond the jurisdiction of the Temperance Societies, we might venture to take a nightcap, and then to bed.

We were roused at dawn by the cheering call of the bugle and the responding notes of the dogs, rushing from their places of rest—the young huntsmen were up—the horses were ready, and soon were we. But before starting we were required to take what the Captain called a *stirrup,* and then pushed forward, passing rapidly over some ground where there was danger of getting up a deer; and let off the dogs upon Simmons's—then moved on to the north. The air was bracing, and the earth shrouded in the most splendid frost I ever beheld—entered Wedden's old field, and paused a while on the side of a hill where the

sun had spread its benign beams. Below us stood the forest, already proud of its morning jewels, and lighting up from the rays of the sun its millions of lamps in rapid succession; presenting a scene so beautiful and interesting that the eye for a short time wandered beyond the influence of the heart, but, like the magnetic needle which had fluttered from the grasp of its controlling power, soon returned, a captive to its point again. Our dogs were now traversing the field with spirit and animation. Damon attracted our notice particularly, scampering down the logs and along the small traces around brier patches, brushing with his nose every rock and chunk, and never for a moment far from the most likely places for a track to be found. While attending to the actions of Damon, we heard at some distance, in the direction of the dry pond, Belmon dropping out his old-fashioned long, trembling note, and saw, at the same time, Jack Falstaff, his brother, hastening on to join him. We thought probably it might be the scent of a deer. Having my gun along, I rode over to him—Echo and Jack had united with him by that time—and on coming in view of them, discovered that it was without doubt the drag of a fox and one that something could be made of. The main pack, however, soon after hit upon the same drag, ahead. I harked up immediately, the dogs with me, and in a little while the whole pack were united, and pushing it forward in the direction of Brown's with life and spirit, having not a doubt of an early start. Every dog was doing his part well; but what gave us all the greatest pleasure was in discovering that poor Crazy Kate was in her right mind.

Our young huntsmen were now dashing after the pack, except one. Him we missed, who never but once before was known to be behind; we soon, however, saw him rushing through the bushes on foot, for he had lost his horse. The pack at this moment was in a full sweep, crossing the road, and bearing to the north under the west side of Rick's fence, and the huntsmen charging, under a belief that the fox would break within the enclosure. I dismounted and gave my horse to the young huntsman on foot, firmly believing that in doing so I should save the life of a man; for he would have broken his heart in the chase, long before the dogs could break the heart of the fox. He was mounted in an instant, and in so much greater hurry than the horse that he rode almost upon his neck; and in coming to the fence, though a fine rider, came nigh charging himself over, while the horse remained on the other side till a few more rails should be let down. At this moment I heard the bold rush of the dogs and the loud and animated shout of C., "He is up." The huntsmen thundered over the plain—the slaves of the farm threw in their cheerful halloos—the flocks of the field crowded back—the horned cattle, more bold, curled their tails and rushed forward to the eminence—gazed a while, then scampered off with fear and delight.

Capt. J——, having, through mistaken calculation, thrown himself a little out, came dashing down the road with his saddlebags drumming to the time of the horse's feet. I told him that he carried too much sail; he agreed, and gave me his bags, of which I was glad; for I knew well what they contained—on he went. The northern enclosure of the plantation brought up all the huntsmen, and by that time the game had doubled and taken his course to the south, in the direction I was standing. The pack approached under a full swell and with the swiftness of the wind; the fox had got across, near Brown's corner without my seeing him; but the hounds were sweeping over the rising ground before me in full view. I saw Crazy Kate and Belmon abreast, leading the pack in beautiful style; then I raised a shout and flourished my bags high in the air. The huntsmen soon appeared in a string through Rick's field; the silver greys riding like Trojans: thinks I, it is well I am out of the scrape, for I see this would have been no day for me to pluck laurels. The fox bore around and threatened to cross again the road—was seen and pronounced to be a very large fox, with remarkably long legs; but the chase soon turned to the east, meandering down, towards town, till I could scarcely hear the cry of the dogs.

I went up to Brown's, found the old lady standing out at the fence, with her silver locks shining in the sun like the frost that morning upon the trees, listening with the utmost apparent interest and anxiety, exclaimed as soon as she saw me, "Heaven grant this may be the day when that fox shall die; to see under yonder fence the feathers of my poultry, one would think the British had certainly been among them, the like," she said, "was never seen before." I told her that if she would fry me an egg and slice of ham, I would ensure his death, and that although I had sail enough in my bags, I could not make a good run without ballast. A breakfast was never got in quicker time. I was soon

again upon the road, wiping my mouth as I went—got down opposite to the dry pond, when I could hear distinctly the chase which had drawn much nearer; but doubling over and over again about Roberts's plantation—discovered that old Jack Falstaff was doing his part well. Thinks I, this is one of Jack's fighting days—Crazy Kate still in her right mind—Yellow Rose playing her octave flute with effect, to horns, bugles and trumpets. At length the chase bore away and stretched along to the west again, on the north side of the Hillsborough road, and soon entered Rick's farm, under a mighty swell—Belmon ahead, Crazy Kate brushing his heels, Rose high up, and Jolly disputing with Yorrick every inch of the ground, old Rock down about Roberts's, where he had much work to do, and likely to be detained several hours.

At this interesting moment my hour had arrived. To turn upon such a scene was a sore conflict; but it would never do to forfeit a sporting engagement; it will be setting too bad an example. I was then several miles from the Fallen Tree, and had to lay my course through woods the whole of the way, without a path. I trotted down the hills and walked as fast as I could up them—soon found myself at the place appointed, and scarcely had time to take one of Sancho's gazes (to avoid too sudden a check of the profuse perspiration I was then in, for the day had in a very short time become very warm) before I heard the deer pack approaching from the south, at a great distance, their notes resembling much the cry of a flock of wild geese, drawing nigh very fast, and in a few minutes after heard with surprise, and delight also, the fox chase bearing down upon Rencher's, near where I was then standing. Ah, what a day, thinks I, this will be to me; I shall down a deer—perhaps there will be two, take one with each barrel, stick their tails on my cap, run down and join the fox chase—succeed in taking the brush, mounting it in my cap, *crow over the silver greys; and then will I flourish my bags in good earnest,* and what a tale will I have to tell Mr. Skinner. The deer pack continued to approach till not a doubt remained of a shot but finally, contrary to all expectation, bore away towards Mrs. Watson's. I ran at top speed to Rencher's Corner, thinking the deer would endeavour to steal his way out there, like on a former occasion. My hopes were vain; he had forced his way through Mrs. W's plantation and cleared himself to the west.

I pushed into Rencher's to join the fox chase, but it had hushed; saw a coloured man who told me the dogs had stopped suddenly near Mr. Hill's, and soon after he saw a huntsman cantering slowly up the creek in that direction; supposed the fox was killed. Thus, Mr. Editor, all my fine castles, built the moment before, were prostrated. I returned and joined the deer huntsman who was then blowing his horn down the log path. When he discovered that I was afoot, dismounted and insisted upon my taking his horse, which I consented to without much persuasion, for I had not quite got over the thumps from my run to Rencher's Corner. We came on together to Captain H———r's, where we met the fox hunters, all chapfallen, and learned with astonishment that the fox had not been taken; they appeared not less so than myself. It was nearly wound up at Mr. H's, when his dogs ran in ahead of the pack, overrun the fox and threw out every dog, and could not again be taken off. The loss happened at the time when the heavy frost of the morning was passing off, which is always a critical moment in a chase; but nothing seemed to surprise the huntsmen so much as the length of time the fox held up, under a press which they thought would have killed nine out of ten in fifty minutes.

The running of the whole of the dogs was highly complimented, except Jack Falstaff, who after distinguishing himself for three hours in the chase, one of the huntsmen having seen the fox, harked up the pack, old Jack looking upon this as foul play and unhuntsman-like, came into the path and cocked his leg against the first stump, and not another stroke would he strike—like his master, perhaps, finding that he would be beaten, was glad of an excuse to get out of the scrape. Old Rock, if he keeps on, will probably arrive at the place where the main stitch was dropped about a week hence; Crazy Kate, Juno, Yellow Rose, and Speckled Flora were most distinguished for their indefatigable exertions to get off the trail at the final loss.

In conclusion of the account of the above chase, I have only to add that although entirely unsuccessful, yet it was one which afforded a vast deal of sport. The weather was fine and the chase lay upon the most favourable ground for the huntsmen, not one of them scarcely for a moment out of sight of the dogs; and I am happy to inform you that the silver greys came out with sound bones, and according to the account given by the young huntsmen, conducted themselves in the most gallant manner throughout the whole affair.

HAWKEYE. *

---

* *American Turf Register*, I, 446–450 (May, 1830).

Deer Hunting

H.

The letter to the *Turf Register* from "H" describing deer hunting is primarily an anecdote, obviously based on a real occurrence, but its preliminary paragraphs provide further indication of the attitude of the Southern gentry toward their field sports. Horsemanship and dexterity in shooting, the writer indicates, were the prime elements in the pursuit of game in the portion of North Carolina where he lived. On the other hand, the reference to baiting a field and shooting game from a scaffold belies the allegation. The conflict in attitudes may be reconciled by the reminder that hunting with horses was apparently regarded as a more genteel sport, one which called for a closer adherence to the rules of gentility. When a huntsman was after meat, that was quite another matter.

The mention of a scaffold built to serve the purposes of the hunter is not common, but there is no reason to believe that such devices were rare. Pits, deadfalls, and scaffolds were all used pretty generally in the Southern region, as they were elsewhere.

Haywood, Chatham Co., N.C., January, 1830

DESIROUS of complying with your request, soliciting communications from sportsmen of the result of their hunting, I have waited, with no ordinary anxiety, during the catching of upwards of thirty foxes, each time hoping the next chase would afford something worthy to record in your very valuable pages, and as often being disappointed, few of that number having stood before our pack more than half an hour before being run into. I abandon, therefore, in despair, the hope of giving you the result of any entertaining fox chase; but, supposing it may not be wholly uninteresting to that portion of your readers, who are alive to the animating cry of dogs, to know the different modes of deer hunting in the different parts of our country, I send you an account of a late hunt during three days. I would here remark that in the part of the county in which I reside deer are not killed with the view wholly to venison, nor that the lucky huntsman should add to his count, but we are only emulous in superior horsemanship in heading the deer oftenest before he is run into by the dogs, or in dexterity in shooting.

The first day, the sportsmen having assembled, being all well mounted, and armed with a short barrel flint and steel gun (percussion being considered dangerous in the eager pursuit of the dogs, from explosion, by striking against trees and bushes), we rode about four miles to a drive, where all entering with the dogs, a challenge was soon given, and a cold trail pursued about a mile, when the whole pack went rapidly off in full cry. We now pursued, under spur, in the direction of Rocky River, for about three miles, when, to our great satisfaction, we discovered the cry to be returning in a direction a little below us. Great exertions were now made to intercept the game in his effort to gain Haw River, but all we could do was only to procure us the sight of a fine buck, at a distance, beyond the reach of our guns, bounding over the low bushes, and struggling to avoid the cry of ten couple of fine dogs, who were pressing him in a style that would have given satisfaction to Nimrod himself. The dogs soon passed us, and we were content to follow at a more moderate gait, hoping to overtake him at Haw River (a distance of about six miles), to which stream he was evidently bending his course; but on our arrival we found, to our mortification, that the pack had there overtaken him, and, as we conjectured, sunk him. The next morning we met, according to appointment, and entering a drive, near Haw River, a challenge and start were successively obtained, and each sportsman pursued the dogs a considerable distance up Haw River, where we were all brought together by the view halloo of one of our party, who, in the pursuit, discovered a buck making his way from Haw River to Deep River. On arriving at the latter stream, the pack swam over, and very soon took the track on the opposite side, and, pursuing it about five miles into the piney woods, forced the buck back again into Deep River, where, after about two hours hard running, he was shot—the whole pack close at his heels. The third morning we again

met, and, after two or three ineffectual efforts, we at length succeeded in arousing a fine doe, which, after a rapid run of about two hours, was ran into by the whole pack in her attempt to gain Buckhorn Creek.

Another mode practised to kill deer with us is exemplified in the following: One of my neighbours discovered that some deer resorted to a small wheat patch, about a mile from him, and determined to kill one or more of them. He accordingly baited a place, and finding the deer regularly came thereto, he erected a scaffold, about ten feet high, in a situation most convenient to the bait and the part of the fence over which they were accustomed to jump into the field. The evening for killing the big buck, as he was called, was at length determined on, and my neighbour, on leaving his house with his old musket heavily charged, told his son that about sunset he might bring down to the baited field the horse and slide, to bring home the big buck and other deer which he might kill, that he need not wait his return, for the game was sure; not having failed to come into the field for some time. He arrived at the place without any occurrence worthy of remark, and, having seated himself advantageously on his scaffold, patiently waited the approach of the big buck.

At length the object of his long labours appeared, and, bounding over the fence, was followed by a second and a third. My neighbour was now highly elated, either of the three being within reach of his shot. Being a large fat man, weighing something like 240 lbs., he was not satisfied with less than all three; and that he might get them all in a range, and have a full load for the slide home, with his musket to his face, ready for the bloody work of death, he took step after step to the right, with as much ease, truly, as the generality of dancing masters, of his weight and in his situation, would have done; but, in his anxiety, he forgot the scaffold had an end, over which he stepped, and down he came, scaffold and all! But, Mr. Editor, this was not the worst of it; my neighbour had his thigh broken, and the deer, by this time, discovering there was some design against them, bounded off into the forest, and left him, without even the consolation of a sight of them, under his affliction. The family at home were all equally sanguine that the big buck was doomed to death, and the son, at the appointed hour, repaired to the wrecked scaffold, under which the father lay, and, cautiously approaching it, repeatedly inquired of the father, "Where was the deer? I have brought the slide."

"Don't talk of deer to me!" vociferated the father, writhing under pain, "put me into the slide, if you can"; so the son assisted the father to get into the slide, and Dobbin was made to draw slowly home. On ascending the hill, near the house, the wife and children all ran to meet the big buck, as they supposed, exclaiming, "Daddy's got the big buck; daddy's got the big buck!—see how hard Dobbin pulls!" But lo, Mr. Editor, you must imagine their disappointment, when, instead of the big buck, my neighbour was in the slide. The inquiries of the children after the big buck was only put an end to by the exclamation of the father, "Don't talk of the big buck to me!"—Now, Mr. Editor, it is true the deer were not killed this time, but you see clearly they might have been.

H. *

* *American Turf Register,* II, 86–88 (Oct., 1830).

Davy Crockett Shoots Bears

DAVID CROCKETT

Hunting bears was an occupation usually practiced by the Southern gentry solely as a means of exterminating varmints, but it was a favorite sport with the humble frontiersmen whose dogs boasted no pedigrees or elevated price tags. Accounts of bear hunting in the South, however, had a tendency to border on the marvelous, for, like the snake, the bear was a favorite animal in folklore. Apparently, the best seasons for the sport were at "lopping time" or "holing time"—when the animals broke off the ends of oak branches to get at the acorns or when they were fattened for the hibernating period. Their skins were of use in making rugs, blankets, and winter caps; and bear oil was employed not only to soften leather and to grease squeaky axles, but to slick down masculine hair and keep primitive lamps supplied with fuel. Where venison was scarce the meat, salted or fresh, was eaten, and even relished, by many folk on the frontier, to whom bear bacon was a kind of household staple. Like deer testicles or conch soup, the flesh of an old bruin, moreover, was thought to restore a man's sexual powers.

The most famous Southern hunting yarn of the twentieth century is William Faulkner's "The Bear"; and two of the most celebrated hunters of all time were exceedingly fond of the sport. One of them not only commemorated a catch uniquely by carving a record of his success on a tree but is said to have had a hand in killing forty or fifty bears on one extensive hunt in 1798. Even more famous than Daniel Boone as a pursuer of the shaggy creatures, however, was Davy Crockett, American bear hunter par excellence.

Long before his death he was a folk hero, his adventures so intertwined with fiction that a common expression was current:

"a sin to Davy Crockett"—meaning anything of an exceptional or extraordinary kind. Beginning in 1834, various more or less spurious "autobiographies" attributed to him were published, and, of course, bear hunting was one of their main features. The following yarn comes from such a source. It was probably ghosted by a journalist, but the substance in all likelihood was based on the yarns with which Crockett had regaled his auditors in legislative corridors or from the platform. His occasional garnishing with humorous exaggeration is well illustrated in the selection by his description of a unique method of avoiding freezing. Such tall tales became typical of the humor of the Old Southwest.

IN the morning I left my son at the camp, and we started on towards the harricane; and when we had went about a mile, we started a very large bear, but we got along mighty slow on account of the cracks in the earth occasioned by the earthquakes. We, however, made out to keep in hearing of the dogs for about three miles, and then we came to the harricane. Here we had to quit our horses, as old Nick himself couldn't have got through it without sneaking it along in the form that he put on, to make a fool of our old grandmother Eve. By this time several of my dogs had got tired and come back; but we went ahead on foot for some little time in the harricane, when we met a bear coming straight to us, and not more than twenty or thirty yards off. I started my tired dogs after him, and McDaniel pursued them, and I went on to where my other dogs were. I had seen the track of the bear they were after, and I knowed he was a screamer. I followed on to about the middle of the harricane, but my dogs pursued him so close that they made him climb an old stump about twenty feet high. I got in shooting distance of him and fired, but I was all over in such a flutter from fatigue and running that I couldn't hold steady; but, however, I broke his shoulder, and he fell. I run up and loaded my gun as quick as possible, and shot him again and killed him. When I went to take out my knife to butcher him, I found I had lost it in coming through the harricane. The vines and briers was so thick that I would sometimes have to get down and crawl like a varment to get through at all; and a vine had, as I supposed, caught in the handle and pulled it out. While I was standing and studying what to do, my friend came to me. He had followed my trail through the harricane, and had found my knife, which was mighty good news to me; as a hunter hates the worst in the world to lose a good dog, or any part of his hunting tools. I now left McDaniel to butcher the bear, and I went after our horses, and brought them as near as the nature of the case would allow. I then took our bags, and went back to where he was; and when we had skinned the bear, we fleeced off the fat and carried it to our horses at several loads. We then packed it up on our horses, and had a heavy pack of it on each one. We now started and went on till about sunset, when I concluded we must be near our camp; so I hollered and my son answered me, and we moved on in the direction to the camp. We had gone but a little way when I heard my dogs make a warm start again; and I jumped down from my horse and gave him up to my friend, and told him I would follow them. He went on to the camp, and I went ahead after my dogs with all my might for a considerable distance, till at last night came on. The woods were very rough and hilly, and all covered over with cane.

I now was compelled to move on more slowly; and was frequently falling over logs, and into the cracks made by the earthquakes, so that I was very much afraid I would break my gun. However, I went on about three miles, when I came to a good big creek, which I waded. It was very cold, and the creek was about knee-deep; but I felt no great inconvenience from it just then, as I was all over wet with sweat from running, and I felt hot enough. After I got over this creek and out of the cane, which was very thick on all our creeks, I listened for my dogs. I found they had either treed or brought the bear to a stop, as they continued barking in the same place. I pushed on as near in the direction of the noise as I could, till I found the hill was too steep for me to climb, and so I backed and went down the creek some distance, till I came to a hollow, and then took up that, till I came to a place where I could climb up the hill. It was mighty dark, and was difficult to see my way, or anything else. When I got up the hill, I found I had passed the dogs; and so I turned and went to them. I found, when I got there, they had treed the bear in a large forked poplar, and it was setting in the fork.

I could see the lump, but not plain enough to shoot with any certainty, as there was no moonlight; and so I set in to hunting for some dry brush to make me a light; but I could find none, though I could find that the ground was torn mightily to pieces by the cracks.

At last I thought I could shoot by guess and kill him; so I pointed as near the lump as I could and fired away. But the bear didn't come; he only clumb up higher, and got out on a limb, which helped me to see him better. I now loaded up again and fired, but this time he didn't move at all. I commenced loading for a third time, but the first thing I knowed the bear was down among my dogs, and they were fighting all around me. I had my big butcher in my belt, and I had a pair of dressed buckskin breeches on. So I took out my knife, and stood determined, if he should get hold of me, to defend myself in the best way I could. I stood there for some time, and could now and then see a white dog I had, but the rest of them and the bear, which were dark colored, I couldn't see at all, it was so miserable dark. They still fought around me, and sometimes within three feet of me; but at last the bear got down into one of the cracks that the earthquakes had made in the ground, about four feet deep, and I could tell the biting end of him by the hollering of my dogs. So I took my gun and pushed the muzzle of it about till I thought I had it against the main part of his body and fired; but it happened to be only the fleshy part of his foreleg. With this he jumped out of the crack, and he and the dogs had another hard fight around me, as before. At last, however, they forced him back into the crack again, as he was when I had shot.

I had laid down my gun in the dark, and I now began to hunt for it; and, while hunting, I got hold of a pole, and I concluded I would punch him awhile with that. I did so, and when I would punch him the dogs would jump in on him, when he would bite them badly, and they would jump out again. I concluded, as he would take punching so patiently, it might be that he would lie still enough for me to get down in the crack and feel slowly along till I could find the right place to give him a dig with my butcher. So I got down, and my dogs got in before him and kept his head towards them, till I got along easily up to him; and placing my hand on his rump, felt for his shoulder, just behind which I intended to stick him. I made a lunge with my long knife, and fortu-

nately stuck him right through the heart, at which he just sank down, and I crawled out in a hurry. In a little time my dogs all come out too, and seemed satisfied, which was the way they always had of telling me that they had finished him.

I suffered very much that night with cold, as my leather breeches, and everything else I had on, was wet and frozen. But I managed to get my bear out of this crack after several hard trials, and so I butchered him and laid down to try to sleep. But my fire was very bad, and I couldn't find anything that would burn well to make it any better; and so I concluded I should freeze if I didn't warm myself in some way by exercise. So I got up and hollered awhile, and then I would just jump up and down with all my might and throw myself into all sorts of motions. But all this wouldn't do; for my blood was now getting cold, and the chills coming all over me. I was so tired, too, that I could hardly walk; but I thought I would do the best I could to save my life, and then, if I died, nobody would be to blame. So I went to a tree about two feet through, and not a limb on it for thirty feet, and I would climb up to the limbs, and then lock my arms together around it and slide down to the bottom again. This would make the insides of my legs and arms feel mighty warm and good. I continued this till daylight in the morning, and how often I clumb up my tree and slid down I don't know, but I reckon at least a hundred times.

In the morning I got my bear hung up so as to be safe, and then set out to hunt for my camp. I found it after awhile, and McDaniel and my son were very much rejoiced to see me get back, for they were about to give me up for lost. We got our breakfasts, and then secured our meat by building a high scaffold and covering it over. We had no fear of its spoiling, for the weather was so cold that it couldn't.

We now started after my other bear, which had caused me so much trouble and suffering; and before we got him, we got a start after another, and took him also. We went on to the creek I had crossed the night before and camped, and then went to where my bear was that I had killed in the crack. When we examined the place, McDaniel said he wouldn't have gone into it, as I did, for all the bears in the woods.

We then took the meat down to our camp and salted it, and also the last one we had killed, intending in the morning to make a hunt in the harricane again.

We prepared for resting that night, and I can assure the reader I was in need of it. We had laid down by our fire, and about ten o'clock there came a most terrible earthquake, which shook the earth so, that we were rocked about like we had been in a cradle. We were very much alarmed; for though we were accustomed to feel earthquakes, we were now right in the region which had been torn to pieces by them in 1812, and we thought it might take a notion and swallow us up, like the big fish did Jonah.

In the morning we packed up and moved to the harricane, where we made another camp, and turned out that evening and killed a very large bear, which made eight we had now killed in this hunt.

The next morning we entered the harricane again, and in a little or no time my dogs were in full cry. We pursued them, and soon came to a thick cane-brake, in which they had stopp'd their bear. We got up close to him, as the cane was so thick that we couldn't see more than a few feet. Here I made my friend hold the cane a little open with his gun till I shot the bear, which was a mighty large one. I killed him dead in his tracks. We got him out and butchered him, and in a little time started another and killed him, which now made ten we had killed; and we knowed we couldn't pack any more home, as we had only five horses along; therefore we returned to camp and salted up all our meat, to be ready for a start homeward next morning.

The morning came, and we packed our horses with the meat, and had as much as they could possibly carry, and sure enough cut out for home. It was about thirty miles, and we reached home the second day. I had now accommodated my neighbor with meat enough to do him, and had killed in all, up to that time, fifty-eight bears, during the fall and winter.

As soon as the time come for them to quit their houses and come out again in the spring, I took a notion to hunt a little more, and in about one month I killed forty-seven more, which made one hundred and five bears which I had killed in less than one year from that time.*

---

* *Life of Col. David Crockett, Written by Himself,* Philadelphia, 1859, pp. 150–157.

Mike Hooter's Bar Story
A Yazoo Sketch

A MISSOURIAN

The "Missourian" who fathered this sketch may have been a writer named William Hall, but we can only guess at the ascription. While it is hardly consonant with the main purpose of the present volume, it nevertheless illustrates an important development in the evolution of the Southern hunting yarn. We can see in it how the humorous exaggerations of Davy Crockett and his ilk became a staple with the increasing tribe of writers who presented themselves to the generation prior to the Civil War more as mirthmakers than as huntsmen. Mike Hooter, who appeared in several other Yazoo sketches of the time, was a forerunner of Petroleum Vesuvius Nasby, Artemus Ward, Bill Nye, and Uncle Remus. Their dialect was a consequential ingredient, and the rage of its popularity now seems almost incredible. For a time the backwoods of the lower South was a favorite locale for such humor, and hunting a relished element. With the enormous vogue of T. B. Thorpe's "The Big Bear of Arkansas" (1841), Bruin came into his own with the "funny fellows."

Like many another similar piece, "Mike Hooter's Bar Story" first appeared in the periodicals but soon found its way into such collections as *Polly Peablossom's Wedding and Other Tales,* edited by Thomas A. Burke and published in Philadelphia in 1851.

IT'S no use talkin'," said Mike, " 'bout your Polar Bar, and your Grisly Bar, and all that sort er varmont what you read about. They ain't no whar, for the big black customer that circumlocutes down in our neck o' woods beats 'em all hollow. I've heard of some monsus explites kicked up by the brown bars, sich as totein off a yoke o' oxen, and eatin' humans raw, and all that kind o' thing; and Capten Parry tells us a yarn 'bout a big white bar, what 'muses hisself climin' up the North Pole and slides down to keep his hide warm; but all that ain't a circumstance to what I've saw.

"You see," continued Mike, "there's no countin' on them varmonts as I's been usened to, for they comes as near bein' human critters as anything I ever see what doesn't talk. Why, if you was to hear anybody else tell 'bout the bar-fights I've had, you wouldn't b'leeve 'em, and if I wasn't a preacher, and could not lie none, I'd keep my fly-trap shot 'tell the day of judgment.

"I've heard folks say as how bars cannot think like other human critters, and that they does all the sly tricks what they does, from instink. Golly! what a lie! You tell me one of 'em don't know when you've got a gun, and when you ain't? Just wait a minit, an' my privit 'pinion is, when you've hearn me thro' you'll talk t'other side of your mouth.

"You see, one day, long time ago, 'fore britches come in fashion, I made a 'pointment with Ike Hamberlin the steam doctor, to go out next Sunday to seek whom we couldn't kill, a bar, for you know bacon was skace, and so was money, and them fellers down in Mechanicsburg wouldn't sell on 'tick, so we had to 'pend on the varmints for a livin'.

"Speakin' of Mechanicsburg, the people down in that ar mud-hole ain't to be beat nowhere this side o' Christmas. I've hearn o' mean folks in my time, an' I've preached 'bout 'em a few; but ever sense that feller, Bonnel, sold me a pint of red-eye whiskey—an' half ov it backer juice—for a coon-skin, an' then guv me a brass picayune fur change, I've stopped talkin'. Why, that chap was closer than the bark on a hickory tree; an' ef I hadn't hearn Parson Dilly say so, I'd ov swore it wasn't er fac, he was cotch one day stealin' acorns from a blind hog. Did you ever hear how that hoss-fly died? Well, never mind. It was too bad to talk 'bout, but heap too good for him.

"But that ain't what I was spoutin' 'bout. As I was sayin' afore, we had to 'pend on the varmints fur a livin'. Well, Ike Hamberlin, you see, was always sorter jubous o' me, kase I kilt more bar nor he did; an', as I was sayin', I made a 'pointment with Ike to go out huntin'. Then, Ike, he thought he'd be kinder smart, and beat 'Old Preach' (as them Cole boys usen to call me), so, as soon as day crack he hollered up his puppies, an' put! I spied what he was 'bout, fur I hearn him laffin' to one o' his niggers 'bout it the night afore—so, I told my gal Sal to fill my private tickler full o' the old 'raw,' and then fixed up an' tramped on arter him, but didn't take none o' my dogs. Ike hadn't got fur into the cane, 'fore the dogs they 'gan to whine an' turn up the har on ther backs; an', bime-by, they all tucked tail, an' sorter sidled back to whar he was stanin'. 'Sick him!' says Ike, but the cussed critters wouldn't hunt a lick. I soon diskivered what was the matter, for I kalkilated them curs o' hisn wasn't worth shucks in a bar fight—so, I know'd thar was bar 'bout, if I didn't see no sine.

"Well, Ike he coaxed the dogs, an' the more he coaxed the more they

wouldn't go, an' when he found coaxin' wouldn't do, then he scolded and called 'em some of the hardest names ever you hearn, but the tarnation critters wouldn't budge a peg. When he found they wouldn't hunt no how he could fix it, he begin a cussin'. He didn't know I was thar. If he had er suspicioned it, he'd no more swore than he'd dar'd to kiss my Sal on er washin' day; for you see both on us belonged to the same church, and Ike was class-leader. I thought I should er flummuxed! The dogs they sidled back, an' Ike he cussed; an' I lay down an' rolled an' laughed sorter easy to myself, 'til I was so full I thort I should er bust my biler! I never see ennything so funny in all my life! There was I layin' down behind er log, fit to split, an' there was the dogs with their tails the wrong end down, an' there was Ike a rarin' an' er pitchin'—er rippin' an' er tarrin'—an' er cussin' wus nor a steamboat cap'n! I tell you it fairly made my har' stan' on eend! I never see er customer so riled afore in all my born days! yes I did too, once—only once. It was that feller Arch Coony, what used to oversee for old Ben Roach. Didn't you know that ar' hossfly? He's a few! well he is. Jewhilliken, how he could whip er nigger! and swar! whew! Didn't you ever hear him swar? I tell you, all the sailors an' French parrots in Orleans ain't a patchin' to him. I hearn him let hisself out one day, an' I pledge my word he cussed 'nuff to send twenty preachers like old Joe Slater an' Parson Holcom an' them kind er Jewdases right kerplumpus into h——, an' what was wus, it was all 'bout nothin', for he warn't mad a wrinkle. But all that ain't neither here nor thar. But, as I was sayin' afore, the dogs they smelt bar sine, an' wouldn't budge a peg, an' arter Ike had almost cussed the bark off'n a dog-wood saplin' by, he lent his old flint lock rifle up agin it, and then he pealed off his old blanket an' laid her down, too. I diskivered mischief was er cumin, fur I never see a critter show rathy like he did. Torectly I see him walk down to the creek bottom, 'bout fifty years from where his gun was, and then he 'gin pickin' up rocks an' slingin' um at the dogs like bringer! Cracky! didn't he linkit into um? It minded me o' David whalin' Goliah, it did. If you'd er seed him, and hearn them holler, you'd er thought he'd er knocked the nigh sites off'n every mother's son of 'em!

"But that ain't the fun yet. While Ike was er lammin' the dogs, I hearn the alfiredest crackin' in the cane, an' I looked up, and thar was one of the eternalest whollopin' bars cummin' crack, crack, crack, through the cane an' kerslesh over the creek, and stopped right plumb slap up whar Ike's gun was. Torectly he tuck hold er the ole shooter, an' I thought I see him tinkerin' 'bout the lock, an' kinder whislin', and blowin' into it. I was 'stonished, I tell you, but I wanted to see Ike outdone so bad that I lay low and kep' dark, an' in about a minit Ike got done lickin' the dogs, an' went to git his gun. Jeemeny, criminy! If you'd only bin whar I was! I do think Ike was the maddest man that ever stuck an axe into a tree, for his har stuck rite strait up, and his eyes glared like two dogwood blossoms! But the bar didn't seem to care shucks for him, for he jist sot the old rifle rite back agin the saplin', and walked off on his hind legs jist like any human. Then, you see, I 'gin to get sorter jelus, and sez I to myself, 'Mister Bar,' sez I, 'the place whar you's er stanin' ain't prezactly healthy, an' if you don't wabble off from thar purty soon, Mizis Bar will be a widder, by gum!' With that, Ike grabbed up ole Mizis Rifle, and tuk most pertickler aim at him, and by hokey, she snapped! Now, sez I, 'Mister Bar, go it, or he'll make bacon of you!' But the varmint didn't wink, but stood still as a post, with the thumb of his right paw on the eend of his smeller, and wiglin' his t'other finger thus (and Mike went through with the gyration). All this time Ike he stood thar like a fool, er snappin' and her snappin', an' the bar he lookin' kinder quare like, out er the corner o' his eye, an' sorter laffin at him. Torectly I see Ike take down the ole shooter, and kinder kersamine the lock, an' when he done that, he laid her on his shoulder, and shook his fist at the bar, and walked toward home, an' the bar he shuk his fist, an' went into the cane brake, and then I cum off."

Here all the Yazoo boys expressed great anxiety to know the reason why Ike's gun didn't fire. "Let's licker fust," said Mike, "an' if you don't caterpillar, you can shoot me. Why, you see," concluded he, "the long and short of it is this, that the bar in our neck o' woods has a little human in um, an' this feller know'd as much about a gun as I do 'bout preachin'; so when Ike was lickin' the dogs, he jest blowed all the powder outen the pan, an' to make all safe, he tuk the flint out too, and that's the way he warn't skeered when Ike was snappin at him."*

---

* *Polly Peablossom's Wedding and Other Tales*, ed. Thomas A. Burke, Philadelphia, 1851, pp. 49–54.

A Bear Hunt
in the Iron Mountain

CHARLES B. COALE

Charles B. Coale (1807–1879) was a Marylander by birth who moved to Virginia and in 1837 became an assistant on the Abington *Virginian,* a weekly newspaper with which he was connected as editor or proprietor for thirty-six years. He was greatly interested in the local history of his section and took an active part in the founding of Martha Washington College. Wilburn Waters, the huntsman mentioned in Coale's story of the Iron Mountain bear hunt, was a local celebrity known as "the hermit-hunter of White Top Mountain." A quarter-breed Indian, born in North Carolina in 1812, Waters became so closely identified with his stamping ground that to the present day his name is mentioned to the tourists who travel on the Blue Ridge Parkway near the Peaks of the Otter, an area of surpassing beauty still thinly populated.

Late in the sixties Waters left his lonely mountain but still continued to hunt in its neighborhood. His yarns, or those told by the choice spirits who were invited to share his company, were first transmitted by Coale through the medium of his newspaper. In 1878 they were reprinted as a book, *The Life and Adventures of Wilburn Waters,* combining local history and the exploits of the old sportsman. The volume was, in turn, reprinted at Abington in 1929, under the title *Annals of Southwest Virginia, 1769–1800,* edited by Louis P. Summers.

THE following was related to the writer by a friend who took his first and last bear-hunt with Wilburn Waters some years ago.

Happening to be in Wilburn's dominions one snowy November, something less than a dozen years ago, and feeling that I could trust my steel-barrel rifle in almost any emergency, as well as having a desire to knock up the trotters of one bear during a residence of an ordinary lifetime within sight of their foraging-grounds, I had the temerity, without due and sober reflection, to ask him if he couldn't get up a chunk of a hunt for my special benefit. "Oh, yes," he replied, "there are two pretty good ones in the laurel across the ridge yonder—I saw the sign yesterday—and if you will take a stand on a branch of the mountain in the morning, I'll hustle 'em up and drive 'em out to you."

"All right," said I, "but, Wilburn, I want you to remember that I am a novice in bear-craft, and you must be careful not to send out too many at once." "Don't be uneasy," said he, "as one will be about as many as you can manage, and I shouldn't be surprised if you don't think that he is *one too many* before you are done with him, for they're awful troublesome critters sometimes."

The hunt being determined upon and arranged, we had bear-meat, corn-dodgers and wild honey for supper, and the long ride through the rarefied air of the mountains that day having whetted my appetite to a pretty keen edge, and having stowed too large a portion under my vest, I was fighting, shooting at, and running from bears the livelong night, in my troubled dreams, and rose from my bed of skins in the morning with very serious misgivings as to the wisdom of bear-hunts in general, and of the present one in particular. But, having of my own free will and accord proposed it, and Wilburn having cheerfully and promptly acceded to it, I had no alternative but to "screw my courage to the sticking point," and go into it whether I got the bear or the bear should get me. We had an early breakfast, but somehow or other my appetite was not as sharp as it was the night before, when I thought of what a dangerous animal a hunted and maddened bear was, and which I could not dispel by more than one libation of "mountain dew" which I usually carried with me in my rambles, *as an antidote for snake bites!*

Everything being ready, we swung our accoutrements around us, threw our guns across our shoulders, Wilburn whistled up his dogs, and off we started. For the first mile or two he diverted my thoughts by instructing me how to act in presence of bruin, and how and where to shoot as he approached me, during which time I stepped along lightly enough, and paid but little attention to the spurs and cliffs over and around which we had been climbing; but after walking along thus for about four miles, the laurel in which the bears held their revel came in view, when all at once, though not without serious premonitory symptoms, my feet began to feel exceedingly heavy, and I entertained very solemn doubts as to whether there was so *very* much sport in bear-hunting after all, particularly where the chances were about equal of being eaten or to eat—the difference, if any, in my opinion, being rather in favor of the bear. My spirits, too, began to flag very perceptibly, and though I tried, I could not attribute my feelings to the weather, for, although the earth was covered with snow, the morning was bright and balmy, the sun shone out in all his splendor, and the crystallized dew-drops hanging upon the foliage of the tall hemlocks, sparkled like gems in the tresses of an oriental bride. The redbirds, all dressed in crimson sheen, flitted in happy glee from spray to spray, the squirrels played their wild gambols among the bespangled tree-tops, and all living creatures around me seemed to be as happy as a bevy of holiday-dressed children at a Sabbath-school festival. I, however, had no relish for the grand and beautiful, for of all animated nature in the wildwood that lovely morning, I alone was to run the risk of being eaten by a bear!

At length we came to the place where I was to take my stand. It was a wild, silent spot upon the mountainside, a few paces from the edge of the laurel where bears "most do congregate," and as soon as Wilburn left me and disappeared in the jungle, I began to feel very uncomfortable—a sort of weakness about the waistbands of my pants—and very earnestly reasoned with myself whether or not it was right and proper to stand behind a tree and murder an innocent bear in cold blood while going about his legitimate business! The more I thought about it the worse I felt, until my knees grew singularly weak, and if I didn't have an old-fashioned shake of ague, it was something so near akin to it that I couldn't well tell the difference; but when, a few minutes later, the perspiration broke out all over me in great big beads, I was ready to be qualified that I had the real *bona fide* Arkansas fever and ague, and thought it not only in very bad taste, but criminally imprudent, for a

man in such a wretched state of health as I was at that moment to be standing away out there on the mountainside without a physician, or quinine, or a bottle of French brandy.

Whilst ruminating upon my condition, and the more serious probabilities of killing a bear or of a bear killing me—in which I had a very decided choice, notwithstanding the maxim that "it is a bad rule that don't work both ways"—I heard the bay of Wilburn's dogs in the distance, and all at once the skin of my head felt as tight as a raw hide on a banjo, and it seemed to me that I would never be able to shut my eyes again, though I never had better reason to keep them as wide open as possible. I would have felt more comfortable under an oystershell at the bottom of the ocean. Looking and listening with the most intense interest, I heard the tread of something coming that seemed to be as heavy as the march of an elephant, and I felt as if I had taken a new lease of life when the formidable animal proved to be a *boomer,* a species of mountain squirrel. Whilst wondering how so small an animal could make so big a racket, I heard the report of Wilburn's rifle away down in the jungle, and my heart raised in thankfulness with the hope that there was one bear less to make a dinner off my bones that day. Another report soon followed, which instead of relieving my anxiety in like ratio, suggested the apprehension that Wilburn, instead of killing a bear, had probably only wounded one, and if so, and he should come across me on his way to the cliffs above, I had better be preparing my nerves for a steady aim, or saying my prayers, or perhaps both. With this unwelcome thought intruding itself, I grasped my rifle with a tenacity that a young earthquake could scarcely have shaken loose, and with a determination that nothing but desperation could have imparted, and awaited the coming of the last thing I wanted to see on the face of this green earth—the very bear I had gone out voluntarily and purposely to kill! While standing thus with one foot rather *unsteadily* planted in front, the breech of the rifle to my shoulder, and my eye running along the barrel, a hand was laid upon my shoulder from behind, and a voice, which I at once recognized as Wilburn's, said, in the sweetest tones to which I had ever listened—"*Stop, friend, hadn't you better spring your triggers and cock your gun before you shoot?*—but you needn't waste your ammunition; I've killed two bears down in the laurel, and there isn't another within ten miles of here!"

If I ever felt happier in my life I have forgotten the time, place and circumstances; my knees became firm and steady; I was all right about the waistband; the cold sweat had vanished like the dew of the morning; I could open and shut my eyes with the facility of a frog, and have not felt a symptom of fever and ague from that day to this.*

---

* Charles B. Coale, *The Life and Adventures of Wilburn Waters, The Famous Hunter and Trapper of White Top Mountain,* Richmond, 1878, pp. 73–82.

Bear Hunt in Louisiana

CHÊNE VERT

The final account, from an unknown writer, is another sample of letters sent to the *American Turf Register.* Because the author throws in an off-hand allusion to *Candide* and signs himself "Chêne Vert," we are tempted to guess that he was a Creole. Like several similar letters included in this volume, the account suggests that the gentry of the Old South—in the present instance, of the bayou country—often knew their literature as well as their guns, dogs, and horses.

"Chêne Vert's" reference to a gentleman from Mississippi who imported stag hounds from the pack owned by the Earl of Derby comes as no surprise, however, for the breeding of hunting dogs was a matter of general concern and the exchange of stock across the Atlantic was a fairly regular practice, although not as common as the importation of horses.

Live Oaks, October 1st, 1829

TAKING it for granted that a bear hunt must necessarily have some interest for your shooters of woodcock, quail, and "such small jeer," if from nothing else than its novelty, I shall proceed to detail to you a morning's sport in that way which I enjoyed a couple of weeks since; premising merely that it took place on the Bayou Grand Caillou, a few miles from the shore of the Gulf, and in one of the best countries for fishing, fowling and hunting in the United States.

Passing through a corn-field about half a mile from my house, I noticed a large quantity of the half ripe corn broken down, half eaten and scattered in every direction over the ground. As I was reflecting upon the cause of this devastation, I accidentally saw the depredator slipping off very quietly, and apparently without observing me, into an adjoining canebrake, in the shape of a large bear. I moved off, as quietly in the opposite direction, and immediately returned home to make preparations for pursuit. After buckling on my hunting knife, and charging each barrel of my gun (one of the Constable's best big bore) with sixteen buck shot each, I called up my dogs, and as they came up, each joining in a howling concert with the horn, could not but be struck with their resemblance to the pack of the powerful Baron Thunder-ten-Tronckh, in Voltaire's romance of *Candide.* They consisted of a couple of noble stag hounds, the sire and dam of which were imported from the Earl of Derby's pack, near Liverpool, by a gentleman of Mississippi; a Scotch wire-haired terrier, not inferior in game and spirit to that Napoleon of small dogs, the far-famed "Billy," so noted in the "annals" of rat-catching; a grey-hound slut, more remarkable for her beauty than her courage or utility; a large and very powerful Spanish dog, of the kind used in the West-India islands to hunt the maroons or runaway slaves, and there called the blood-hound, though bearing no resemblance to the ancient slot or sleuth hound, more frequently called the blood-hound, used in the olden time to follow up the trail of thieves in the Scotch highlands; and a bull-mastiff, sufficiently large and powerful to pull down an ox. To these were added all the watch and stock dogs of the plantation, "Tray, Blanche and Sweetheart, little dogs and all,"—adding much to the numerical, though little to the actual strength of the gang, for it hardly deserved the name of pack.

Upon reaching the spot, where I had a few minutes before observed the corn was broken down, the hounds instantly hit off the trail, and broke into the canebrake at a round rate, making their full mellow cry ring through the woods, and followed by the whole pack perfectly silent, except an occasional yelp from some of the younger members of the family. By the way, I cannot help stopping to ask, though not altogether apropos to the subject, if it is not because men are naturally created hunters, as is evinced by their having little other employment in the barbarous ages of the world, that every man, whatever may be his creed, philosophy or pursuit, feels a strong glow of pleasurable excitement upon hearing a pack of hounds, "full-mouthed, broad-chested and dew-lapped like Thessalian bulls," making the hills and woodlands ring with their enlivening cry. But *revenons á nos moutons.*

Finding the game had gone off in a direction parallel to the open ground, I pushed off in a rapid canter, in order to get ahead of both bear and dogs, which I easily accomplished, owing to the thick canebrake obstructing their course in a very great degree. I dismounted and crowded through the cane, till I reached some open ground, here and there obstructed only by an occasional palmetto, and soon had the pleasure of hearing not only the hounds, but the whole tribe of curs yelping most vigorously, and making directly towards the point where I stood. A moment after, I heard a strong rustling and cracking in the cane, and in an instant Bruin leaped into the open ground, close followed by the greyhound and terrier, the one from her extreme activity, and the other from his small size being able to slip through the cane quicker than the other dogs. The bear was very large, and apparently fat, and from his open mouth seemed much out of wind. He had scarce freed himself from the cane before the greyhound gave him a severe pinch in the haunch, which made him instantly turn, though she had no difficulty in avoiding him—as he again started to run, the terrier seized him behind, but not relinquishing his hold soon enough, the bear turned and threw himself directly upon him. I started and ran with all speed toward the animal, cocking my gun as I went; for though not more than sixty yards, I was too distant to fire with effect upon so large a creature with buck-shot, and thinking all the time, that the poor terrier Beppo had hunted his last hunt—but whether owing to the bear's alarm at my approach, or the dog's diminutive size preventing his readily seizing him, I know not, but he escaped without the slightest injury.

By this time he was surrounded by the whole pack of dogs, and though bitten on every side, thought it best to beat a rapid retreat. I would have fired, but reflecting that I was running quite as much risk of killing my dogs as the game, I hesitated to do so. After he had run about forty yards, the bull-mastiff seized him by the ear or cheek, and was so strong as to nearly throw him; as he fell he grasped poor Nero, who gave a single sharp cry before he was hugged to death, having, as I afterwards found, nearly all the ribs on one side completely crushed in. The bear kept on in an awkward but pretty rapid canter, occasionally turning to drive back the dogs, when they pushed him too hard, till he was out of sight. I followed, and after going about half a mile, had the pleasure of finding, from the cry of the dogs, that he was at bay. Upon coming up, I found Sir Bruin sitting upon his posteriors, with great gravity, in an angle formed by two fallen trees, with a semi-circle of dogs in front, occasionally striking at them with his paws, as they now and then approached nearer than he thought proper. I was now within five and twenty yards distance, and partly concealed by some small bushes, when it struck me that if I drew my shot and replaced them by a bullet, I should by killing him almost instantly, prevent his injuring the dogs, an accident which very rarely fails to happen when a bear is only severely wounded. I accordingly drew the shot, and had just driven home the bullet, when the terrier and some of the small curs, getting round the logs which protected my Russian friend in the rear, crept under them and seized him, "in the part, where honour's lodged," as wise philosophers have judged, in a manner that put them entirely out of his reach, and again compelled him to start on his travels. Finding that the open ground gave a great advantage to the dogs, he again made for the thick canebrake. Three of the dogs were very much crippled by blows, which they had received, though only one of them had his skin broken, this was the Spanish dog; naturally extremely ferocious, and unaccustomed to hunting the bear, he aimed all his attacks at the head and throat, which exposed him much more than the other and more experienced dogs, who rarely or never attempt to seize the bear except when running, and then invariably aim at his hinder parts.

At this stage of the chase, I was joined by a neighbour, who hearing my dogs, soon brought up a reinforcement of curs, which, after following the bear in a semi-circle for about a mile, pushed him so hard as to compel him to take to a tree. Upon reaching the spot I found my neighbour, who being less fatigued, or a little lighter on the hoof, had outrun me, was just upon the point of shooting. He had one of the small bored rifles used in Kentucky and the adjoining states for shooting squirrels and wild turkeys, carrying one hundred and ten balls to the pound. For the purpose of rendering this small bullet effective, he aimed at the eye, with the intention of entering the brain; in this, however, he failed, as the ball struck about half an inch above the eye, on a hard

long ridge which glanced it upwards and left it, as we afterwards found, about three inches from where it entered, perfectly flattened, between the scalp and the skull. The shock produced very little effect upon the animal, as he did not change his position,—he merely shook his head and gave a low growl, while the blood trickled freely from the end of his nose. He was crouched with his head downward, and toward me upon a large limb of a live-oak, which put out at nearly a right angle to the trunk, and about sixteen feet from the ground.

I approached within thirty feet of him, took aim very deliberately, and drove a bullet, weighing something more than an ounce, directly into his breast, which passed, as I afterwards ascertained, through his heart and lodged against the spine. He pitched forward and fell very heavily upon the ground, and was instantly seized by the dogs, who pinned him so fast, as to enable me to thrust my hunting knife up to the handle in his chest, which soon put an end to his struggles. We immediately sent off for a cart and bore him home in triumph. After taking off the skin and dressing the carcass, we found it to weigh two hundred and sixty-seven pounds; at least eighty of which were pure fat.

As regards the best kind of dog for bear hunting, I am disposed to think that a cross between the common deer- or fox-hound and the Spanish blood-hound spoken of above would prove the best, as there would be nose enough on one side, and ferocity and strength enough on the other. Yours, respectfully,

CHÊNE VERT.*

---

* *American Turf Register,* I, 237–240 (Jan., 1830).

www.ingramcontent.com/pod-product-compliance
Lightning Source LLC
Chambersburg PA
CBHW080733230426
43665CB00020B/2721